R

The M

AD

Developing
Skills

DATE DUE

Robert S. Weinberg, P
North Texas State University

Demco, Inc. 38-293

Leisure Press
Champaign, Illinois

loging-in-Publication Data

The mental ADvantage.

Bibliography: p.
  Includes index.
    1. Tennis--Psychological aspects.   I. Title.
GV1002.9.P75W45   1988   796.342'01'9   87-3722
ISBN 0-88011-293-X

Developmental Editor: Judy Patterson Wright, PhD; **Copy Editor:** Claire Mount; **Assistant Editors:** Janet Beals and JoAnne Cline; **Production Director:** Ernie Noa; **Projects Manager:** Lezli Harris; **Typesetter:** Yvonne Winsor; **Text Design:** Keith Blomberg; **Text Layout:** Denise Peters; **Cover Design:** Keith Blomberg; **Cover Photo:** Bill Morrow; **Illustrations By:** John Evanko and Shannon Bryant-Hankes; **Printed By:** Versa Press

ISBN: 0-88011-293-X

Printed in the United States of America   10   9

Leisure Press
A Division of Human Kinetics
Web site: http://www.humankinetics.com/

United States: Human Kinetics, P.O. Box 5076, Champaign, IL 61825-5076
1-800-747-4457
e-mail: humank@hkusa.com

Canada: Human Kinetics, Box 24040, Windsor, ON N8Y 4Y9
1-800-465-7301 (in Canada only)
e-mail: humank@hkcanada.com

Europe: Human Kinetics, P.O. Box IW14, Leeds LS16 6TR, United Kingdom
(44) 1132 781708
e-mail: humank@hkeurope.com

Australia: Human Kinetics, 57A Price Avenue, Lower Mitcham, South Australia 5062
(08) 277 1555
e-mail: humank@hkaustralia.com

New Zealand: Human Kinetics, P.O. Box 105-231, Auckland 1
(09) 523 3462
e-mail: humank@hknewz.com

Dedication

To my wife Kathleen, our children Josh and Kira, and both our families.

Acknowledgments

The writing of a book is not merely the result of one individual's effort. Rather, it involves the assistance, concern and encouragement of many people and I would like to acknowledge these contributions.

Lorna Bryua for typing and retyping the manuscript.

Howard Zelaznik for his helpful comments on an earlier draft of the manuscript.

Judy Wright for her thoughtful and insightful comments on the manuscript as my developmental editor.

Shannon Bryant-Hankes for her creative artwork.

Coach Steve Buck and the North Texas State Tennis Team for their cooperation in posing for the tennis-action photographs.

All the tennis players and coaches I have worked with over the last several years for their insights on the mental side of tennis.

My family and friends for their constant support and encouragement.

Quotation and Photo Acknowledgments

Credit is given for quotations taken from the following sources:

pp. 12, 13, 15, 16, 17, 19, 24, 25, 26, 27, 30, 57, 61, 74, 76, 77, 87, 127, 128, 130, 135, 138, 139, 142-143, 163, 167, 177, Barry Tarshis, excerpted from *Tennis and the Mind*. Copyright © 1977 Barry Tarshis. Reprinted with the permission of Atheneum Publishers, Inc.

pp. 165-166, 179, Quote permission Golf Digest/Tennis, Inc. From the book, *If I'm the Better Player, Why Can't I Win?*, by Allen Fox. Copyright © 1979.

pp. 20, 74, From *The Inner Game of Tennis*, by W. Timothy Gallwey. Copyright © 1974 by W. Timothy Gallwey. Reprinted by permission of Random House, Inc.

Table 8.1, pp. 106-109, Adapted by permission from "Imagery in Sport" by Rainer Martens, an unpublished paper presented at the Medical and Scientific Aspects of Elitism in Sport Conference, Brisbane, Australia (1982, September).

Credit is given for interior photographs taken from the following sources:

pp. 11, 57, 73, 89, 99, and 145, used with permission from Jack L. Groppel (1984). *Tennis for Advanced Players*, Champaign, IL: Human Kinetics Publishers, Inc.

pp. 1, 23, 39, 115, 127, 163, 177, 189, Center for Instructional Services, North Texas State University.

Contents

Preface

Tennis is a game that can be fun, exciting, and challenging. You can also experience frustration, anger, and failure on the tennis court. Whether you achieve the former or the latter usually depends on your mental approach to the game rather than your physical ability. That is not to say that physical ability is unimportant, rather it has been a common practice to exclusively work on the physical aspects of the game and ignore the mental aspects. Most tennis books, instructional camps, teaching pros, and coaches emphasize the physical side of the game. You can learn about body mechanics, footwork, weight transfer, angles of return, topspin, slice, stroke production, and so on in almost any tennis book or magazine you pick up. But where can you learn about the mental aspects of tennis?

That is where the idea for this book began. My experience as a tennis player, coach, and sport psychologist made me realize the importance of the mental side of tennis. In observing and playing in many tennis matches, I began to realize that the player with better strokes, form, footwork, and coordination did not necessarily win the match. Players with superior physical skills would invariably walk off the tennis court in disbelief, mumbling to themselves "How could he possibly beat me? He doesn't have any strokes." But that is just the point. Nice strokes do not necessarily win tennis matches; it takes a total effort and commitment to endure highly competitive tennis matches. In essence, the struggle on a tennis court is both physical and mental. The mental struggle is not necessarily against an opponent. Rather, it is a struggle that goes on inside ourselves, and if we can win the mental game, the result will usually be not only better performance but more enjoyment and fun.

Another way to demonstrate the importance of the mental game is to look at our day-to-day performance. There are some days when everything flows and we hit the ball really well with good pace and accuracy. Then there are other days when we can't seem to do anything right on the court. Do we suddenly lose the skills we've acquired over many years of practice? The answer to this is obviously no. We are probably experiencing changes in our mental and emotional state and because of this we lack confidence as well as the motivation to play or concentrate from day to day. Although we don't lose the ability to hit our serve overnight, the ability to control our thoughts and emotions can certainly change both from day to day and within a match.

In recent years, I have presented numerous workshops and seminars to tennis players and coaches. These participants all agree that, although the mental side of the game is extremely important, they usually spend little time on this aspect simply because they don't know how to practice psychological skills such as controlling anxiety, improving concentration, building confidence, and enhancing motivation. Most players and coaches, however, are eager to learn more about the elusive mental game but do not know where to go to get this information. This need and interest convinced me of the necessity of a book that focused on the mental side of tennis. I was also convinced that the book should be action-oriented, providing specific exercises, techniques, and strategies to practice and improve mental skills. The major objectives of the book are:

1. To educate tennis players and coaches about the importance of psychological training for achieving tennis excellence, thus motivating them to teach or train in this area.
2. To describe the psychological states associated with peak performance in tennis.
3. To discuss the development of psychological skills (e.g., anxiety management, concentration, imagery, confidence, self-talk, goal setting) to help tennis players reach their full potential.
4. To detail specific techniques, strategies, and programs to practice developing these skills.
5. To demonstrate that developing psychological skills will lead to not only better performance but also greater enjoyment and fun on the tennis court.

Introduction

Over the past 25 years, more and more scientific evidence has attested to the integration of mind and body. More specifically, research has indicated that one's mental state can have enormous impact on his or her physiological state. In fact, many of our autonomic nervous system reactions (e.g., heart rate, skin temperature, muscle tension, etc.) which were once believed to be out of our conscious control have been shown to be strongly affected by our thoughts and mental state. Similarly, our state of mind has proven to be an important mediator of how we perceive and cope with pain as well as how quickly we recover from surgery and illness. In essence we are just beginning to realize that the mind has been a virtually untapped reservoir in terms of its relationship and control over many bodily functions and processes. On the average, we use only a small fraction of our mental potential; there is limitless potential yet to be discovered and released.

In a similar fashion, the relationship between mental state and physical performance has been a concern for coaches and athletes for a long time; and yet, until recently, little research has been conducted. Although most tennis coaches and players allude to the importance of the mental side of sports, they spend little or no time training their mental ability. Jimmy Connors recently said that tennis is 95% mental at the professional level. He reasoned that because all professional players have great physical ability, (e.g., strokes, quickness, coordination) what separates the winners from the losers is the mental aspect of the game. This is true for tennis players of all levels, from juniors through masters, because most of us seek out competitors similar to us in terms of physical skills, age, and conditioning. When the physical aspect of the game is equalized, the mental aspect becomes critical in determining not only who wins and loses but how satisfied we are with the quality of our playing. When we walk off the tennis court mumbling to ourselves that we played terribly and never should have lost, we are really talking about the mental side of our game. The major premise of this book is that neither mastery of tennis skills nor satisfaction can be accomplished without paying attention to the mental game of tennis. The mental game is critical when tennis players fight against nervousness, lapses in concentration, self-doubt, and self-criticism. It is this aspect that tennis players and coaches need to work on, develop, and refine. The time has come to direct our attention to winning the mental game. The material in this book is based on the latest research from sport psychology as well as the experience of coaches and players concerning their experience with the mental game. I have also included my own work on developing psychological skills in tennis players to provide a solid foundation of how to go about improving one's mental game.

Chapter 1 emphasizes the importance of the mental game. As the ability level of two players becomes more equal, the mental aspects of the game become more critical in determining the eventual winner and loser. Also, because of the way the game of tennis is scored, one or two points can make the difference between a 6-4, 6-4 win or 6-4, 6-4 loss. Thus, the importance of staying mentally tough throughout a match is critical to success. Chapter 2 describes the psychological states that tennis players associate with their top or peak performances. There is a constellation of thoughts and emotions that is consistently related to top tennis performance across individuals. The goal of the mental game is to develop the capability to consistently produce these positive thoughts and emotions. To win the mental game, however, requires practicing and learning psychological skills such as anxiety management, concentration, self-talk, imagery, confidence, and goal setting; these are discussed in chapters 3 through 11.

Specifically, chapter 3 discusses the sources of anxiety and how excess anxiety can cause both physical and mental problems. The relationship between anxiety and performance is presented along with the concept of achieving an optimal arousal level. In chapter 4, a variety of relaxation and stress-reduction techniques are presented to cope with excess anxiety both on and off the court. In addition, techniques for psyching-up or increasing arousal are discussed.

Chapter 5 provides a foundation for understanding concentration or attentional focus. Various problems concerning achieving and maintaining proper attentional focus are presented. In addition, the chapter discusses the importance of focusing on the relevant cues during a match while eliminating distractions such as crowd noise and opponents' antics. Chapter 6 presents several techniques or exercises for improving concentration and provides a variety of on-court tips to help you keep your mind on the match instead of focusing on irrelevant cues. Central to good concentration is having positive as opposed to negative self-talk; this is the focus of chapter 7. As a tennis player, you have lots of time to talk to yourself between points and the things you say have a profound impact on your subsequent performance. Statements such as "You stink," "What an idiot you are," "I hope I don't choke again," and "How can you be so bad?" will deteriorate rather than improve performance. Statements like "Hang in there," "One mistake doesn't mean a match," "Just watch the ball," and "I can beat this player," will usually have a positive influence on performance.

Chapter 8 discusses the concept of imagery which is one of the most talked about subjects in sport psychology in the 1980's. The different types of imagery and their usage are described along with how imagery works. The chapter emphasizes the importance of getting a vivid, controllable image by using all your senses. Chapter 9 provides a step-by-step approach to implementing an imagery training program. Exercises are designed to use at home, in the preparation for matches, and during matches. Certain time periods are highlighted as especially good ones at which to employ imagery: before serving, receiving serve, and changeovers.

Chapter 10 introduces the psychological skill of confidence. Although many people believe that confidence cannot be taught, research has demonstrated that it can be. In fact, confidence has been found to be the best psychological discriminator between successful and less successful athletes. When you lack confidence you psychologically limit youself and are not likely to reach your potential, despite your physical abilities. Ways to enhance your confidence are provided; also, the concept of being overconfident is explored because this can result in losing matches that you should have won.

Chapter 11 presents the final psychological skill of goal setting. If you are not highly motivated and enthusiastic, then all of the things discussed in the previous chapters will probably not matter that much. One of the most potent ways to enhance your motivation and subsequent performance is through goal setting. Goal setting is not the answer in and of itself, however, because there are a number of principles to follow to maximize its effectiveness. Therefore, a list of goal setting principles are discussed which concern both practice and match situations. In addition, chapter 11 provides a detailed description for coaches of establishing a goal setting program and carrying it out.

Chapters 1 through 11 have hopefully laid the foundation for developing the psychological skills necessary to win the mental game. With these skills, you should be able to deal effectively with most situations that arise in the course of a tennis match. There are some additional practical situations to consider, however, to round out your approach to winning the mental game.

Chapter 12 approaches the important subject of preparing for a match. Although many of the previous chapters have addressed this subject, this chapter closely examines preparing for a match both psychologically and physically. The idea is to progressively get the mind and body focused and prepared as the match draws nearer. Bad preparation usually produces bad results. Chapter 13 addresses the important but often overlooked area of gamesmanship and psychological strategy. Learning how to deal with your opponent's psychological ploys during the warm-up and match helps you to gain psychological control of yourself and the match. Gamesmanship is usually not taught or written about, but you need to be aware of the different types of games people play and how to cope effectively with them. Finally, chapter 14 highlights the psychology of doubles. Although many of the concepts, principles, and techniques discussed in the book can be applied to doubles, the big difference is that you have to interact and communicate with a partner. From a psychological point of view, the key to a good doubles team is effective communication. Unfortunately, many of us are not skilled in the art of communication; this results in problems on the tennis court. Several suggestions are offered for improving both verbal and nonverbal communication between partners. Finally, the unique case of mixed doubles is addressed including the special problems that arise in this situation.

By reading this book you demonstrate that you are serious about and interested in improving your game. It is hoped that the skills you learn will help you win the mental game. You will not always walk off the court a winner, but you will be able to effectively control your thoughts and emotions on the court. If you can achieve this end, then you will have gone a long way to reaching your physical potential as well as getting more enjoyment and fun out of the game. It is not necessarily an easy journey, but it is a worthwhile pursuit. Have a nice trip.

CHAPTER 1

How Important Is the Mental Side of Tennis?

Have you ever walked off the tennis court in disgust because you lost a match that you felt you should have won? Have you ever choked at a critical point in a match? Have you ever become upset over a bad line call and lost your concentration? Have you ever lacked the desire or motivation to practice or get ready for a match? Does your mind ever wander and think about other things during a match? Have you ever become tentative and started to push the ball on important points in a match? Have you ever become angry and frustrated with your game and thrown your racquet or called yourself names?

If you answered yes to one or more of these questions don't despair because you have a lot of company. In fact, in my experience working with tennis players and coaches it has been extremely rare (if not impossible) to find a tennis player who does not fall victim, at least at times, to the ravages of the mind. Nobody who has played tennis with any degree of seriousness or passion would dispute the statement that beyond the purely physical and technical aspects of the game is a mental or emotional component that often overshadows or transcends the physical aspects. All of us who play tennis know what it feels like to be ''in the zone'' where everything seems to come together and winners fly effortlessly off our racquets. Conversely, we have all probably had days when nothing went right, we felt tight and uncomfortable, and every shot was an adventure. Although we all know these feelings, few of us can control or understand them.

Why Is Tennis Difficult From a Mental Standpoint?

Why is tennis such a difficult game from a mental standpoint that it drives perfectly rational people to emotional outbursts, swearing, throwing racquets, and the like? First of all, tennis is a very exacting game which requires a precise combination of timing, coordination, quickness, decision making, and stamina. In fact, in the average tennis match, it has been found that a player will have to make approximately 900 to 1,000 decisions, each of which have to be made in less than a second. Second, from a biomechanical point of view, if your racquet face varies by just a couple of degrees this will likely result in hitting the ball into the bottom of the net or out past the baseline. This makes tennis a potentially frustrating game.

Third, and most importantly, the stop and go nature of tennis distinguishes it from many other sports like soccer or basketball in which the action is constant. In essence, tennis presents the mind with lots of dead time (especially between points and changeovers) and this places great stress on the mind. In fact, in a typical tennis match, one-third of the time is actually spent playing tennis, whereas two-thirds of the time is spent between points and changeovers. It is during this dead time that the mind wanders and becomes absorbed in all sorts of distractions ranging from ''I don't want to choke on this second serve'' to ''I wonder what I should wear tonight for the party.'' Tennis forces the mind to make abrupt switches from action to thought; this invariably produces mental errors which in turn produce technical errors in stroke production.

It is just this reason that makes golf such a tough game from a mental standpoint because the golfer is left with lots of time to think after each shot. Similarly, in basketball, it is common practice for a coach to call a timeout just before an opposing player is about to attempt a critical free throw. The coach wants to give the opposing player plenty of time to think about the importance of the shot, hoping his or her mind will start working overtime and get in the way of making a successful free throw. Turning back to tennis, in my coaching, playing, and counseling experience with tennis players, most agree that the two hardest shots to hit from a mental standpoint are the serve and the overhead smash. Although these two shots are certainly difficult from a technical standpoint, what makes them particularly hard is that the player usually has time to think before hitting each shot. This thinking time allows distractions and irrelevant thoughts to enter the mind thereby disrupting timing and coordination. The main point is that tennis puts great pressure on the mind to make exacting decisions under pressure; the dead time puts further stress on the mind to be focused and ready for action. The key, therefore, is to develop a better understanding of how the mind and body can work together.

Relationship Between the Body and Mind

Over the past 25 years, more and more scientific evidence has been accumulating that attests to the integration of mind and body. More specifically, research has indicated that our mental state can have an enormous impact on our physiological state. In fact, many of our autonomic nervous system reactions such as heart rate, temperature, and muscle tension, once believed to be out of our conscious control, have been shown to be strongly affected by our state of mind. For example, with proper training, most of us can be taught to lower the temperature in a particular part of our body or reduce tension in a specific muscle in the body. Additionally, it has been found that the level of stress in our daily lives is linked to the likelihood of illness or disease. In fact, it has been shown that athletes with higher levels of stress are more prone to serious injury. Similarly, our state of mind has proven to be an important mediator of how we perceive and cope with pain as well as how quickly we recover from surgery and illness.

Athletes many times are expected to play with a certain amount of pain and injury. Given the same amount of pain, an athlete who mentally copes with the pain plays more effectively than another athlete who allows the pain to be a distraction from the task at hand. I've seen tennis players play with pain and I didn't know they were hurt until they completed their match, whereas others are visibly distracted by their pain or injury. In essence, we are just beginning to realize that the mind has been a virtually untapped reservoir in terms of its relationship and control over many bodily functions and processes. On the average, we use only a small fraction of our mental potential; there is limitless potential yet to be discovered and released. This is where the mental side of tennis comes into play.

The Mental Side of Tennis

As for the scientific community at large, the relationship between mental state and physical performance has long been a concern for coaches and athletes. In tennis, as in any sport, a player's success (or failure) is attributed to some combination of physical abilities (e.g., speed, strength, coordination, balance, etc.) and mental abilities (e.g., concentration, confidence, and motivation). How important are the mental and physical capabilities of a tennis player for determining success? To answer this question, I have asked both coaches and players in my workshops and seminars to rate the importance of the mental and physical side of tennis. By their own admission, almost all the coaches and players felt that tennis success (i.e., performing up to one's capabilities) was at least 50% mental, with many indicating that it was 80% to 90% mental. These percentages held true in my three-year survey, regardless of the age, gender, or ability of the players. Similarly, as previously noted, in a recent interview, Jimmy Connors stated that he felt tennis was 95% mental at the professional level and of course Connors has long been known for his mental tenacity and toughness.

Another way to look at the importance of the mental side of tennis is to compare two of the greatest women tennis players of all time—Chris Evert and Martina Navratilova. For anyone who has observed the women's professional circuit over the past 10 years, it is common knowledge that Chris Evert is not the best athlete on the tour. Yet, she has been ranked number one in the world for many years and has achieved a record of consistency that has virtually been unsurpassed. If she is not the most physically talented woman on the tour, then what has accounted for her incredible success? The consensus is that nobody is better than Chris Evert mentally. Her concentration has been said to be unwavering regardless of line calls, distractions, or opponent's antics. She plays the big points extremely well and her patience from the baseline is unparalleled. Furthermore, when she fell to number two in the world, she rededicated herself and through her drive and motivation is again a challenger for the number one position.

Conversely, Martina Navratilova has always had incredible physical ability including strength, speed, quickness, and superb shot-making ability, including an overpowering serve and volley game. Yet for several years she continually came up short in the big matches and would make critical mistakes at inopportune times. Most tennis aficionados felt that Martina would never win a major tournament until she learned to better control her thoughts and emotions. To her credit, she had the desire to be the best and worked hard on her mental game. The result of this hard work was the number one ranking in the world along with an incredible string of consecutive victories. Soon, if Martina lost it made national news and the only uncertainty in most of her matches was whether or not she would win in under one hour. Bringing her mental game up to the level of her physical game made her virtually unbeatable.

How Much Time Do You Spend Practicing the Mental Side of Tennis?

The next question I have asked of the workshop and seminar participants is "How much time do you usually spend mentally and physically practicing in a typical week?" Their responses revealed some interesting discrepancies; that is, most competitive tennis players state that they physically practice between 10-20 hours per week (this figure is somewhat lower for the typical club player). The typical response concerning how often they work on their mental game, however, is not at all or for a few minutes before a match. Yet when most players come off the court after a loss, they tend to attribute the loss to psychological factors such as, "I wasn't up for the match today,'' ''I just couldn't concentrate,'' ''I got too tight when the match got close,'' ''I just didn't have any confidence in my shots today,'' or ''I just hate to play in the wind.''

Players and coaches feel not only that the mental side is extremely important, but that it becomes even more critical when physical abilities tend to equal out. That is probably the reason why Jimmy Connors said that 95% of the game is mental at the professional level. He reasons that at the professional level all the players are very talented in terms of physical skill. Of course a few players have exceptional ability or are known for a particular shot—Ivan Lendl (forehand), Jimmy Connors (return of serve), Martina Navratilova (serve and volley), John McEnroe (serve and volley), Chris Evert (backhand)—but in general, there is not a lot of difference between the players in terms of their physical abilities. In fact a large percentage of matches are usually determined by the outcome of a few critical points. For example, in a 1984 match between John McEnroe and Ivan Lendl, the outcome was a seemingly routine 6-4, 6-3, 6-4 victory for McEnroe. A closer inspection reveals, however, that the match was determined by the outcome of some critical points; that is, each player had a total of three break points against his serve throughout the course of the match with one break point in each set. McEnroe won the three break points against his serve and Lendl lost the three break points against his serve, resulting in a straight-set victory for McEnroe. Furthermore, an analysis of the total number of points won in matches often reveals that, in a close match, the losing player actually wins more total points but obviously not enough crucial points.

These ideas are important for all tennis players regardless of their ability, because we all seek out players who are usually fairly similar in ability to ourselves. If you're an ''A'' club player you probably play predominantly with other ''A'' players. If you are a 16-year-old junior ranked in the top 20 in your state you probably compete mostly with other players of your own age and skill level. Of course, there are times when you are clearly over-matched in terms of physical skills or are clearly superior to your opponent. In these cases, the winner of the match will almost always be the player with the most physical skills and shot-making ability. In most of your matches, however, you probably have a good chance of either winning or losing, depending on how you play on that particular day. Why do you play well one day and feel that everything you hit is going to be a winner whereas the next day you are not able to hit a ball over the net? Did you all of a sudden lose your ability to serve or hit a backhand passing shot, or was your mind just getting in the way of allowing you to perform up to your potential? The obvious answer is the latter: you haven't lost your physical skills; rather, it's your mental skills that seem to fluctuate from day to day or even hour to hour.

Why Is the Mental Side Not Practiced?

If both coaches and players alike agree that the mental side of tennis is critical in becoming a successful player, then why is so little time and emphasis put on practicing or developing one's mental or psychological skills? From talking with coaches and players, there appear to be two major reasons why these skills are either not practiced at all or given superficial attention.

Psychological Skills Are Believed to Be Innate

One reason is that it is generally believed that a player either has or does not have psychological skills. A common misconception is that we are somehow born with these mental skills, and that champions are born rather than made. It has often been said that Jimmy Connors was a born fighter who was blessed with a mental toughness and competitive drive that separated him from most other players. Most people would say that it is just part of Connors' personality.

Although it is true that we are all born with some innate predispositions concerning our physical and psychological makeup, it is also true that these abilities can be learned and altered depending on the type of experiences we encounter in our lives. No great tennis players have achieved stardom without dedicating themselves to the game through endless hours of practice, honing these skills and shots. Of course, some players have special talents that are hard if not impossible to teach such as John McEnroe's touch around the net, Bjorn Borg's quickness, Martina Navratilova's serve, or Chris Evert's consistency. All of these players, however, had to work hard to develop their special talents in order to become great champions.

But just as physical skills need to be constantly practiced, so also do psychological skills. The ability to concentrate, relax under pressure, and maintain your confidence when behind needs to be systematically practiced, developed, and integrated with physical skills. These mental skills are neither magically learned nor simply part of a player's make-up. They are indeed *skills* and therefore require a daily training regimen. This is an extremely important point and will be one of the major thrusts of the book. Mental skills need to be practiced just like physical skills if you expect to become a more consistent tennis player. Most players I have been associated with make an occasional stab at practicing mentally but don't expect any significant results from haphazard practice. If you wanted to improve your second serve depth you would probably serve a bucket or two of balls whenever you could. But if you were dissatisfied with your concentration, would you practice improving your concentration skills? If you want results, you have to be willing to put in some time and effort.

Coaches Don't Know How to Teach Psychological Skills

A second reason for the failure of coaches and tennis pros to systematically teach players about the importance of mental skills is that most coaches do not really understand how to teach these skills. Have you ever heard a tennis coach teaching concentration? If you have, it probably sounded something like this: "Will you concentrate out there," or "Will you get your mind on tennis." Of course, this provides no information to tennis players about how to concentrate. Rather, the implicit assumption is that the player knows how to concentrate but is just not doing it. Another common practice is to tell players to just relax on important points or for important matches; once again, this is much easier said than done, particularly without training in relaxation skills. A coach wouldn't expect a player to hit an American twist second serve on break point if the player hadn't practiced that shot extensively. In fact, a player would be foolhardy to try such a shot without proper preparation through hours of practice. Similarly, psychological skills such as concentration and relaxation need to be practiced before they become effective tools in competitive situations.

The above comments are not meant to criticize coaches. The truth is that they work extremely hard with their players to improve their games. Unfortunately, most coaches and players have not had access to techniques and methods for teaching and learning how to improve their psychological skills. This is because the field of Sport Psychology in the United States is just recently evolving to the point where research findings are establishing a scientific basis of knowledge that is just now being applied to competitive athletics. The United States Olympic Committee, for example, has recently recognized the importance of Sport Psychology and is in the midst of establishing formal training programs in many of the Olympic sports, with sport psychologists working with our national teams. Many individual athletes, including professional tennis players, have sought out the assistance of sport psychologists to help solidify and fine-tune their mental approach to tennis.

Although a lot has been happening in the past couple of years in the application of sport psychology principles for enhancing athletic performance, little has been made available to most tennis players and coaches.

As a result, despite the acknowledged importance of the mental side of tennis, usually no more than "lip service" is paid to this aspect of the game. We are constantly told: "Don't choke," "Get psyched-up," "Be mentally tough," "Concentrate," "Stay loose," and "Be confident"; but these carry little meaning in terms of what they really convey to the tennis player. These words need to be translated into an action-oriented approach that provides tennis players with a plan for improving their psychological skills.

Psychological Skills Can Be Learned If Practiced Regularly

This leads us to one of the major purposes of this book; that is, to provide tennis players and coaches who are serious about improving their games with specific ideas, techniques, exercises, and strategies concerning the mental aspects of tennis. I will try to demonstrate that certain psychological states are consistently associated with higher levels of tennis performance. Consistently achieving these psychological states, however, has been a problem for many tennis players. The top players are generally the ones who can control their thoughts and emotions on a consistent basis, which allows them to maintain a high level of excellence from day to day.

The remainder of the book will attempt to provide you with an in-depth approach to developing your psychological skills. Understanding and taking control of your mental game will not only allow you to perform closer to your potential but also make playing tennis an enjoyable and fun experience. The journey is not always an easy one, but the end result will provide you with the mental strength and psychological skills necessary to make your tennis experience not only more successful but also more self-fulfilling.

CHAPTER 2

Psychological States of Successful Tennis Players

There are few things more frustrating in tennis than knowing that you rarely play up to your potential when it really counts. However, sometimes the harder you try to do well the more likely you will fall prey to the ravages of the mind. This initiates a vicious cycle of self-doubt, frustration, anger, self-criticism, and disappointment. The disappointment is usually not so much from losing a match as from knowing that you performed well below your potential.

In working with tennis players of all levels, I constantly hear the same refrain, "I am not playing up to my potential" or "Sometimes I play really well but other times I stink up the court." A quote by the two-time Grand Slam winner, Rod Laver, speaks to the point of how elusive our mental state can be.

You can go out on the court some days and feel so sharp and so alert that the ball comes over the net looking as big as a soccer ball, and you think to yourself that there's no way I can make a mistake. Other days you can go out and play as if you're in a fog, unsure of everything. I can remember a match I played in Spain once against Borg when my mind was miles from the court and I had no real awareness of what I was doing except that I was getting beaten badly. The next day I played doubles and everything was back to normal. Can I explain the difference? I wish I could, but I can't. I can only say that tennis is a game you can never take for granted.[1]

Of course, Rod Laver was "on" most of the time which helped make him one of the greatest champions of all time. But even the greatest players have days when their minds wander and their play becomes erratic. Many tennis players feel that they are on a performance roller coaster with a great performance one day followed by a subpar performance the next. These players often do not know how they will perform on a given day and report that their mental and emotional states seem beyond their conscious control. Although we all, at times, feel out of control on the tennis court, there are many tennis players who never get a handle on their thoughts and emotions. This will usually result in increased frustration; the players eventually will lose whatever interest and competitive drive they once possessed. Juniors are particularly prone to this type of misfortune although it can occur at any age or ability level.

Striving for Consistency

To avoid these pitfalls, it is necessary to become more consistent in your performance; consistency is the key to being a successful tennis player. The distinguishing trademark of players such as Bjorn Borg, Chris Evert, Mats Wilander, Ken Rosewall, and Guillermo Vilas, for example, is not so much their exceptional talent, but rather their exceptional ability to consistently play up to their capabilities. Almost anyone can pull off a big upset on any given day, but can they maintain this level of play for their upcoming opponents? Along these lines, I have spoken to many players who erroneously evaluate their ability based on their best performance, such as beating the number two seed in a tournament or losing in three close sets to a player who later turned pro. The more astute tennis players will realize, however, that they are only as good as their worst, not best, day. In order to win a tournament, a player has to be able to withstand an off day and still find a way to win. The great champions do not let their games fall too much because they know that every match could result in an upset. A great victory is hollow if it's followed by a demoralizing defeat.

To achieve the consistency necessary to play tennis at a high level requires two things. The first is good basic technique, stroke production, and movement. Many tennis players are inconsistent simply because they have not sufficiently refined their strokes. Variability in basic mechanics will lead to inconsistency in one's level of play. Even if you are mentally tough, you will not be able to remove the inconsistencies in your game unless you become more consistent in your stroke production.

The second requirement for achieving a high level of consistency in your performance revolves around your mental and emotional skills. In essence, the extent to which you play with consistency depends on how successful you are in creating and maintaining a stable mental state. Peaks and valleys in performance are many times directly related to psychological inconsistencies. The ability to put yourself in the proper psychological frame of mind and maintain this throughout a match is critical to being a successful tennis player. However, the first stepping stone is finding out what this psychological state should be.

A Special Mental State

I can't remember ever playing a match in which I was so focused on what I was doing and yet so unconscious about it. I was making all the right decisions, but not consciously thinking about them.[2]
Manual Orantes on his 1975 Forest Hills Victory over Jimmy Connors.

I just started to feel so confident in my game. I felt that no matter how hard I hit the ball it was going to go in the court. I was no longer occupied with winning or losing, but rather I was just totally focused on the match.[3]
Ivan Lendl after his victory over John McEnroe in the 1985 U.S. Open.

The above quotes represent two samples of players describing their feelings and thoughts during top moments in their careers. This book could be filled with similar descriptions of other tennis players attempting to recapture the unique feelings and thoughts associated with their best performances. It is interesting to note that when athletes in a variety of sports are asked to describe their top performances, they consistently use the same terminology and feeling states. Whether it came from a tennis player, golfer, swimmer, basketball player, baseball player, archer, or long-distance runner, athletes have reported that a unique psychological state exists when they are performing up to their potential. This mental state is distinctively different from their description of the thoughts and feelings associated with poorer performances.

On a more scientific level, research evidence has been rapidly accumulating that links specific mental and emotional states of athletes during competition with the quality of their performance. The relationship between these special emotional states and exceptional performances is called *flow* or *peak experiences*. In tennis terminology this is commonly called *playing in the zone*. You might think that this involves gritting your teeth and giving 110%. However, playing in the zone usually means that the tennis player is so involved in the immediacy of the experience that he or she allows things to happen instead of trying to make them happen. Attention is directed externally to the immediate environment (e.g., the tennis ball, movements of your opponent) to the virtual exclusion of one's own analytical thinking. In essence, the body is reacting automatically and the player is just letting the body do what it is trained to do. There is no self-doubt, self-criticism, fear of failure, or other distractions, but rather a single-minded, present focus.

A composite of the thoughts and feelings that tennis players report during outstanding or peak performances is presented below:

> *I felt very relaxed but yet I was energized and feeling strong. I enjoyed the tennis competition and was not afraid to lose. In fact, I felt a sense of calmness and quiet inside and my strokes just seemed to flow automatically. I really wasn't thinking about my shots and what I needed to do; it just seemed to happen naturally. My shots did not feel rushed, in fact the ball seemed to slow down and I felt as if I could do almost anything, I was totally into the match but yet I was not consciously trying to concentrate. I was aware of everything but distracted by nothing. I knew my shots were going in and I felt confident and in control.*

Of course, it is unusual for a tennis player to feel all of these things at one point in time, although it has been done. The key is that what is generally called mental toughness is the ability to create and maintain the type of mental state described above. To perform up to your potential requires that you create a particular internal climate and maintain this mental state throughout the course of a match. This special mental state helps bridge the gap between what you *can* do and what you *actually* do as a tennis player. That is, it allows you to perform consistently closer to your potential as a tennis player. You are always your own toughest opponent and until you win the battle inside your mind you will not consistently win the battle against your competition. The good news is that you can control your mental state and create the kind of internal climate that will allow you to get the most out of your physical skills and abilities.

Specific Psychological States

From the responses of thousands of athletes, the following are the psychological states most commonly described as a part of their best performances. The rest of the book will be concerned with helping tennis players achieve these desired psychological states.

Highly Confident

Successful players are distinguished from less successful players by their strong belief in their abilities. This belief transcends any particular match or situation; the confident tennis player remains poised and calm during adversity. This is not to say that they feel confident all of the time. It does mean, however, that they don't lose confidence in themselves and their game despite momentary setbacks. Everyone loses tennis matches and has off days, but the great champions do not let that undermine their genuine belief that they can and will be successful. A couple of quotes will illustrate the central role that confidence plays in one's tennis game.

Stan Smith

When you're not confident it affects nearly everything you do on the court: the way you move, the way you hit the ball, the way you think. You let winning opportunities go by, you tighten up on easy points; it's the catalyst to your entire game. When it goes your game goes.[4]

Brian Gottfried

The difference between feeling confident when you're playing and not feeling confident is that you never hesitate to go for shots and you're not giving your opponent the extra opportunities you give him when you're not feeling confident and you're just trying to keep the ball in play.[5]

If you listen to tennis players describing their good or bad performances, invariably you will hear comments like, "I just didn't have any confidence in my strokes today" or, conversely, "I felt very confident that no matter how hard I hit the ball, it would stay in the court." Without confidence, you will never reach your potential as a tennis player. Although confidence is sometimes an elusive feeling, a successful tennis player must always maintain a positive attitude regardless of the circumstances or opponent. If you go onto the court expecting to perform poorly and not believing you can win then you are setting youself up for failure. Because confidence is such a crucial psychological skill, belonging in the repertoire of every serious tennis player, it is discussed in depth in chapter 10.

Focused Concentration

When tennis players describe their top or peak performances, they invariably report that they were totally focused in on the match. They are unaware of any distractions even to the point of not being aware of the audience or a plane flying overhead. The only thing that matters in the tennis player's world is the moment. There is no worry about what just happened or what might happen. Their world consists of the tennis court, the tennis ball, and their opponent. There is no room for irrelevant thoughts or distractions. A tennis match can last for two or three hours, and one break in concentration can mean the difference between victory and defeat. This point can be seen in the comments of Bjorn Borg.

> *Very often in a tennis match you can point to just one game where for a couple of shots you lost concentration and didn't do the right thing, and the difference in the match will be right there.*[6]

It is interesting to note that many top professionals feel that they rarely respond to conscious acts of trying to concentrate. Tennis players who are performing well typically are not trying to concentrate; rather, concentration just seems to happen naturally. Of course, it will happen naturally more often if you practice on your concentration skills. This idea is supported by Chris Evert who has long been known for her extraordinary concentration skills.

> *Basically, what my dad and I used to do in my practice sessions was to keep hitting as many balls as we could without a miss. With me, concentration developed so naturally that I rarely have to force myself to do it. It's part of my game.*[7]

Concentration is another skill that can be learned and practiced. The longer each point goes and the longer a match goes, the more important concentration becomes. Add onto this things like wind, noise, sun, line calls, and opponent's antics and it becomes obvious that a player without good concentration skills is doomed to failure. For this reason, chapters 5 and 6 are devoted to a discussion of how to improve your concentration skills.

Physically Relaxed

For years, coaches have been trying to psych up their athletes for an upcoming opponent or event. Getting psyched up and ready for a match usually has meant feeling a little tight and nervous. Although it is somewhat natural and even expected for a tennis player to be a little nervous before going out to play an important match, this same muscle tension is detrimental to performance during a match. Research has indicated that tennis players usually perform at their best when they are physically relaxed with a minimum of muscle tension. Tight muscles can cause players to lose the fluidity in their strokes. Instead of hitting out and going for their shots, they become tentative and start to push the ball. Of course, the more pressure there is, the more likely it is that they will tighten up and become tense.

Relaxed muscles are particularly critical in tennis because tennis requires so much fine-muscle coordination, precision, and accuracy. Sports requiring minute adjustments and extraordinary timing are usually adversely affected by even small amounts of muscle tension. For example, if muscle tension in your forearm and wrist causes you not to come over the ball when hitting a topspin forehand or backhand, the ball will likely go too long because topspin requires a loose wrist to impact the proper spin to the ball.

Another potential problem stemming from muscle tension is that it drains your energy; being tense means that your muscles have to work overtime. This can become a serious problem, especially in long matches. Arthur Ashe illustrates this point.

The one thing I've learned about tension on the court that's helped me is something I got from Pancho Gonzales. He told me once that if you can somehow learn to relax in between points, the tension won't build up in a match the way it does if you try to concentrate every second. Physical fatigue can make you mentally tired and whatever you do to minimize the tension will make choking much less likely. [8]

Chapters 3 and 4 are devoted to providing you with a better understanding of how anxiety affects performance. Specific relaxation procedures will be discussed to help you deal with the pressures inherent to competitive tennis.

Effortless

When tennis players describe their best performances they commonly report that everything seemed to flow effortlessly. Rather than indicating that they were not giving 100% effort, this means that the players were not trying too hard. There is a big difference between giving 100% effort and trying too hard. You have to let it happen rather than trying to make it happen. When things start to go badly in a match, the tendency is to try harder and force things. The proper tactic, however, would probably be to ease up and let go. Trying too hard will not only produce increased muscle tension but probably result in a mental state that is unfocused and frantic.

Some of the comments from tennis players reflect this sense of effort-lessness when they are at the top of their game.

I just seemed to be floating out on the court. I was moving well and I just always seemed to be one step ahead of my opponent. My strokes felt smooth and effortless and I was picking up the ball real early.

Everything seemed to move in slow motion. The ball looked as big as a melon and I felt I had all the time in the world to prepare. I wasn't thinking about how to hit my shots but my strokes were crisp and efficient.

Lack of Fear

One of the hardest barriers that tennis players face is the fear of losing. Many tennis players report that thoughts of losing, making mistakes, and

disappointing coaches, friends, and parents as well as letting themselves down occupy their minds before, during, and after matches. When players describe their peak performances, however, they are not preoccupied with what might happen if they miss a shot or lose a match. There is no fear; rather, the player is calm and quiet inside. Because the mind is not pre-occupied with the negative consequences of failure, it can focus on the moment and the task at hand. Many players play not to lose instead of playing to win, and this usually results in tentative play and holding back on their shots. Champions don't fear failure and their games don't suffer from self-doubt and indecisiveness. Chris Evert's following comments demonstrate that fear of failure has never been a factor in her mental attitude.

A lot of it really had to do with the way I was raised. My father was very careful to react pretty much the same way whether I won or lost. When he was critical, it was never because of the outcome of the match but because of certain things I may not have done right. But he was never harsh. I never went into a match afraid of how he would react if I lost.[9]

Automatic

A common theme that characterized most tennis players' descriptions of their top performances is that they seemed to be playing instinctively and automatically. There was no time for thought and analysis, as this tends to get in the way of the proper execution of strokes. This concept of shutting down the mind and putting the body on automatic pilot has received much support in the sport psychology literature and is similar to the approach that Tim Gallwey takes in his popular book *Inner Game of Tennis*. This is not to say that there is no time for thinking in the game of tennis. You obviously need to plan strategy, choose shots, and be aware of opponent's strengths and weaknesses. When the point begins, however, there is no time for the mind to be giving the body instructions. If your strokes have been sufficiently practiced, trying to analyze what you have to do will result in errors and missed opportunities. This has been called *paralysis by analysis*. Trying to tell yourself to keep your elbow tucked in, head locked, knees bent, backswing short, and follow-through high will invariably produce information overload.

The top players know how to turn on the automatic pilot and play predominantly by instinct. Of course, this becomes more difficult depending on how important the match is to you. In high-pressure situations you are more likely to start to think about and analyze the situation. But when a match begins, your mind must remain clear and uncluttered. Between points a simple cue like *forward* or *racquet back early* can be helpful to provide the proper mind-set for the upcoming point. During a point, however, you must leave behind how important the shot is as well as other cues that focus on being critical and evaluative. This point is illustrated by Tim Gallwey.

The least efficient way to do anything with your body is to consciously try to do it. In tennis, the minute you let yourself become too consciously involved with why it's important for you to hit a particular stroke a particular way, or why it's important for you to make a point, you are setting up an obstacle between what you're trying to do and what you have to do in order to hit the shot the way you want to.

Clearly, to play unconsciously does not mean to play without consciousness. That would be quite difficult. In fact, someone playing out of his mind is more aware of the ball, the court, and when necessary, his opponent. But he is not aware of giving himself a lot of instructions, thinking about how to hit the ball, how to correct mistakes, or how to repeat what he just did. He is conscious, but not thinking, not over-trying. A player in this state knows where he wants the ball to go, but he doesn't have to try hard to send it there. It just seems to happen and often with more accuracy than he could have hoped for. The hot streak usually continues until he starts thinking about it and tries to maintain it; as soon as he attempts to exercise control, he loses it. [10]

So when players, after a great match, say, "I was just unconscious out there" or "I just played out of my mind," what are they really saying? By saying that they were unconscious, the players are simply saying that their minds are so concentrated and focused that they can put their bodies on automatic pilot with no interference from thoughts and emotions. One of the goals of this book will be to help each of you reach this state of mind more often.

In Control

Another one of the psychological states that characterizes the peak tennis experience is a sense of being totally in control. You feel that you are controlling the situation, rather than having the situation controlling you. Tennis players who report that they feel in control of their game take personal responsibility for their performances and do not blame things that are out of their control. For example, how many times have you heard tennis players bemoaning the fact that their poor playing or loss was due to too much wind, bad surface, bad luck, bad weather, sun in their eyes, bad line calls, and so on. The thing that all these conditions have in common is that they are beyond the control of the player. When players are in control of the situation, they feel that their actions and play will determine the outcome of the match. They are not concerned with events that are beyond their control, rather, they are confident that they are in control of the situation. For example, players can control their anxiety level, temper, approach to mistakes, and breathing as well as other mental and emotional states. These are psychological skills and they can be learned, as will be demonstrated throughout the book.

Enjoyment-Motivation

As simple and straightforward as it might seem, a high degree of enjoyment and even exhilaration characterizes the peak experiences of tennis players. This sense of enjoyment and fun is strongly tied to a positive mental attitude and feelings of energy. If tennis players do not enjoy the game their future on the court is probably limited. You cannot continue to give 100% effort and energy to your game if you do not enjoy what you're doing.

When Bjorn Borg announced his retirement from the game he said that one of the major reasons for his decision was that he just wasn't enjoying the game anymore and could not motivate himself to be totally dedicated to the game as he had been in the past. To be good at tennis requires a lot of hard work, dedication, and practice; the successful tennis player has to be highly motivated. Thus, when players lose their enjoyment of the game they usually lose their motivation to practice and work hard as well. The result could be what is called *burn-out*. Unfortunately, this is a term we have heard all too often recently in the world of tennis, particularly with younger players. Several of the top young tennis professionals in the United States have had bouts of burn-out as they have questioned their motivation to continue to devote all of their energies to the game. The common theme among these players is that they have temporarily lost their enjoyment of the game due to the intense pressures, travel, rigorous schedules, boring practices, or some combination of the above. This lack of fun and motivation is captured in the following quote by a young tennis player.

I used to look forward to getting up in the morning so I could play tennis. I couldn't wait to get on the tennis court because it was so much fun and I really enjoyed it. But as time passed by it became more and more difficult for me to get motivated to play whether in practice or in a match. I'm not sure if it was the pressure of winning (from my parents, coaches, and myself), the boredom of practice, the same players in the same tournaments, or just my feeling that there are other things in life besides hitting a tennis ball over a net. Whatever the reason, I just lost my spark and enthusiasm and tennis has become a drag— more like work than play.

The Journey Ahead

This chapter has emphasized that consistent, high-level play will most often be accomplished if you can first consistently create the proper internal mental state. When the right internal climate takes form, playing well occurs naturally and spontaneously. This ideal mental state includes the following thoughts and feelings:

- Highly Confident
- Focused Concentration
- Physically Relaxed
- Effortless
- Lack of Fear
- Automatic
- In Control
- Enjoyment-Motivation

This does not mean that you necessarily have to achieve all of these states to play at the top of your game. It does mean, however, that the better you learn how to achieve and maintain these states the more likely you will be to reach your real potential as a tennis player. Of course, as noted previously, it will take some work and effort on your part to learn these mental skills. But just by reading this book you have already demonstrated that you are a serious tennis player and motivated to improve your game.

The primary goal of the rest of the chapters is to help you develop your psychological skills to the point where you can control your mental and emotional states instead of their being in control of you. Being a mentally tough tennis player translates into the ability to create and maintain the proper psychological state regardless of the situation or circumstances. As you have probably heard or realized, it's easy to maintain positive thoughts and feelings when everything is going your way. The real test comes when things get tough, the pressure is high, you're behind, and everything goes wrong. If you can stay relaxed, confident, concentrated, in control, and motivated under adverse conditions, then you are well on your way to winning the mental game. It won't always come easy, but when you get there it will have been one of the most fulfilling journeys of your life.

 **CHAPTER 3**

How Anxiety Can Affect Performance

Sometimes when I go out on the court to play an important match, I get so nervous that I actually have trouble breathing. My strokes feel rigid and forced instead of natural and I feel tension in my forearm and neck. To make matters worse, when I try to run my legs feel stiff and tight and I feel real slow on the court. I start pushing my shots with little or no follow-through. It seems that I lose all my tennis instincts and I am being controlled by the fear of losing.

The above quote probably represents what most of us have felt more than once on a tennis court due to feelings of nervousness and anxiety. Even some of the calmest players in the game such as Arthur Ashe, Chris Evert, and Bjorn Borg have stated that they get nervous and uptight in important matches.

It doesn't really matter whether you are playing in the finals at Wimbledon or in the finals at your local club tournament—the pressure to win can still have an adverse effect on your performance. Hitting a second serve with set point against you, putting away an overhead to win an important game, hitting a passing shot at game point, returning to break serve, and serving for the match are all situations that signal pressure to most tennis players. Wouldn't you rather play these pressure points well instead of becoming tentative and hoping that your opponent will make a mistake?

Consider the comment from Bjorn Borg concerning the pressure of playing the big points, with particular reference to playing Jimmy Connors.

> *Against most players, whenever I need only one more point to win the*
> *set or to break serve, I can hit the ball fairly shallow because most*
> *players will not go for a winner off that shallow shot. They'll tighten*
> *up a little, hit the shot safer and give me a chance to win the point*
> *on the passing shot. But Connors doesn't play safe, he just hits out.*[1]

Of course, Jimmy Connors is noted for his style of play which allows
him to raise the level of his game on important points. He generally does
not succumb to the pressures of the moment. However, with a better
understanding of the nature of anxiety and its physical and psychological
effects on performance as well as some techniques to effectively cope with
our anxieties, you can learn to control your anxiety during the course of
a competitive match. This does not mean that you eliminate anxiety totally;
rather, you learn to manage and channel it more effectively. Before developing this psychological skill you must understand the sources of anxiety
and their effects on tennis performance.

Sources of Anxiety

In a recent survey, over 1,000 athletes from a variety of sports were asked
the following question: ''What is the one thing that has most prevented
you from reaching your potential as an athlete?'' The response given most
often was ''The failure to effectively cope or deal with my anxieties before and during competition.'' This result alone says a lot about the critical role that anxiety plays in achieving maximum performance. To say
that the ability to cope with pressure and anxiety distinguishes the world
class players from other players of similar physical ability might be over-
stating the case, but the following comments by Charlie Pasarell are note-
worthy in this regard.

> *I can think of dozens of players that nobody has ever heard about who*
> *can hit the ball as well and as hard as anybody on the tour but just*
> *can't get it together in a match situation. The reason that guys like*
> *Laver, Newcombe and Connors are champions is that they always do*
> *their best on big points in key situations. Most players, on a big point,*
> *will play it safe, let the other guy make the error. But the other players*
> *aren't afraid to gamble. They'll choke too, every now and then, but*
> *usually they're going to put the pressure on you.*[2]

The ability to raise the level of their game under pressure is certainly a characteristic of world class players. Before I discuss how to manage your anxieties and effectively cope with the pressures of competitive tennis, you first need to understand the sources of stress. The following sources of stress for tennis players have been identified in a variety of research studies conducted over the past several years.

Fear of Failure

The fear of failure is the most prevalent reason given by tennis players for what makes them nervous and anxious. The immediate fear of failure usually revolves around fear of losing a match, missing a shot, looking bad, or losing an important point. But in reality, this is only part of the problem because all of these fears are usually due to more deep-seated insecurities in a person's self-concept or self-esteem. These insecurities are characterized by statements such as, "My ego is really on the line in this match," "What will other people think if I lose?" "I don't want to disappoint my coach or my parents," "I'll never be able to face my friends back at the club if I lose," and "If I lose, everybody will think that I choked."

What these statements have in common is that losing represents a threat to one's self-esteem or self-worth. In essence, a tennis match becomes much more than just a tennis match. The consequences of winning or losing a match are taken far beyond the realms of the tennis court. It is as if you think that somehow you are a better person or will be more well-liked if you win, or conversely, that you are a lesser person or will not be as well-liked if you lose. This of course puts tremendous pressure on you because your ego is so tied to the outcome of the match. Rod Laver, two-time Grand Slam winner, dealt with this fear of failure in the following manner.

> *The thing that always worked best for me whenever I felt I was getting too tense to play good tennis was to simply remind myself that the worst thing—the very worst thing—that could happen to me was that I'd lose a bloody tennis match. That's all.*[3]

Fear of failure usually results in a tennis player playing not to lose instead of playing to win. On the surface this may seem like a minor difference, but it can produce profound differences in the way a player approaches and plays a tennis match. When tennis players are afraid to lose they are usually content to park themselves on the baseline, hit very conservative shots and hope that their opponent will make a mistake. Although this strategy may work to some degree at lower skill levels (especially if the opponent is equally afraid of losing), as players become more experienced and better competitors, they will usually seize the opportunity to pressure their opponent into a mistake. This is not to say that you should just blast away and be very aggressive on important points. In fact, if you are generally a baseline player and are not comfortable or very skillful at net, it might be ill-advised to rush net on key points. For example, Chris Evert has long been known for her baseline consistency. Few people realize, however, that she does become more aggressive on big points and will go for the lines or more depth without taking foolish or unnecessary chances. In addition, as her volley has improved, she has started to rush net more and put more pressure on her opponents at critical junctures in the match. She is not afraid to hit her shots when it counts, and she does not just hope that her opponent will make an unforced error. In essence, she is not afraid of failure.

Unfortunately, not all of us are as cool, calm, and collected as Chris Evert. Playing not to lose is a common problem as noted by Julie Heldman.

Most tennis players don't play to win, they play not to lose. When you play not to lose, you go out and do your best but you don't go beyond that. You're not willing to put yourself on the line and do everything in your power to win. I could never do it. I could play well enough as long as my strokes were doing the job, but when it came down to me having to dominate the other person, I couldn't handle it. And that's what separates most women players from people like Billie Jean King. [4]

Fear of Inadequacy

This source of anxiety is couched in a player's feeling either physically or mentally inadequate for an upcoming opponent or event. It can be based on either real or imaginary competence as well as physical and/or psychological preparation. Although it is somewhat similar to the fear of failure, the fear of inadequacy is specifically characterized by the attitude, "Something is wrong with me," or an attitude that reflects self-depreciation and personal dissatisfaction. In essence, tennis players report that they feel ill at ease due to their inability to properly prepare themselves for the competition. The players reported feeling inadequate or fearful about the following things: inability to concentrate, inability to psych up, lack of desire to play, lack of physical conditioning, not enough rest, and inability to control tension.

It's extremely important that tennis players feel good about their mental and physical preparation for a match. When they feel that they have adequately prepared themselves through their training regimen, then they can approach the match with confidence. As Roy Emerson notes:

Any time you walk on a tennis court in less than top physical shape you're giving yourself a convenient reason for losing. Usually, that's what you'll do. When I was playing the circuit, I knew that there were players on the tour who had better strokes than I, but I had confidence in my body. I knew I had trained harder and prepared myself better than the other guy, and I knew that if it came down to a fifth set, he was more likely to wilt than I was.[5]

Loss of Control

Another characteristic that consistently appeared when tennis players reported their anxieties was not being in control of the situation. As you recall, being in control was one of the psychological states discussed in chapter 2 in relation to achieving peak performance. The concept of control refers to what psychologists call *locus of control*. Individuals who have an *internal* locus of control usually feel that their efforts and actions will, to a large extent, control or at least have an impact on the outcome of a particular situation. Conversely, individuals who have an *external* locus of control believe that they have little or no control over events in their lives. For example, people who have an internal locus of control would feel that if they were well-prepared and did well on a job interview, they would have a good chance of getting the job, whereas people with an external locus of control may not prepare well for the job on the assumption that getting a job is a matter of luck; in this last instance, people feel they have no control over whether they get hired. How does this relate to tennis players?

In translating how loss of control affects a tennis player's anxiety let's look at a few situations or events that many players feel are out of their control. One area in which players feel a loss of control is line calls. I've heard many players attributing their loss to a bad line call (or a series of them) at a critical point. They feel helpless in this situation because they have no control over the calls; this can cause anxiety. Players with more self-control, however, realize that matches are rarely won or lost on a line call and they just have to take the good with the bad. Other players use it as a convenient excuse for losing (i.e., they do not feel responsible for the loss).

Another important situation in which loss of control produces anxiety is weather conditions, particularly the wind. I know many tennis players who are so psyched out when playing in the wind that they lose the match

before they step out onto the court. Refrains such as "I just can't play in the wind," or "I just hate the wind" are not uncommon. Because there is nothing that can be done about the wind, this creates stress, and players agonize over how awful it is to play under such conditions. Of course, the wind exists on both sides of the court, so your opponent must also contend with it. Playing in the wind requires extra concentration; players who feel out of control become so uptight that the wind interferes rather than helps them with their concentration.

Spectators present yet another aspect of the loss of control that can cause apprehension. Most players like to play in front of a supportive, enthusiastic crowd. This may not be the case, however, if you're playing against another school or if you are the favorite to win. The behavior of spectators is, for the most part, beyond your control, but it nonetheless can make you feel tense and anxious. For example, even playing in front of a supportive audience consisting of friends and family may make you nervous because you want to do well and please them and thus you may try too hard. Once again, the thing to remember is that you are in control of how you play, and whoever happens to be in the audience should be of little or no consequence to you.

Of course there are other events that tennis players feel are out of their control and thus produce anxiety. These include the type of playing surface (e.g., clay, asphalt, grass, synthetic), condition of playing surface, temperature, and conduct of your opponent as well as other distractions around the court. Although these things can produce stress, they do not have to, especially if you can learn to effectively cope with them. These coping skills will be emphasized in chapters 4 through 10.

Somatic Complaints

A final indicator of anxiety is called *somatic complaints*. Somatic complaints are the physiological manifestations of anxiety with which we are all quite familiar: rapid heart beat, upset stomach, sweating, tight muscles especially in shoulder and neck, urge to urinate, and shallow respiration or breathing. These are very common symptoms of anxiety not only during a match but particularly before a match. If, however, these physical symptoms are a result of being nervous and apprehensive, then how do they create anxiety? What happens is that players interpret these symptoms, such as rapid pulse or shallow breathing, as signs that they are indeed anxious. Because most tennis players are told that excess anxiety will hinder performance, this in turn makes them more anxious and nervous. The key here is to understand that these physiological signs are normal and are even to be expected when getting ready to play a big match. In fact, it would be quite unusual if you did not experience any of these feelings. The comments of Vic Sexias, one of the all time greats, echoes these thoughts.

Early in my career I read an article that quoted Ted Williams as saying, "I never overcame nervousness." That statement stuck with me throughout my career. I got to the point where I actually wanted my mouth to feel a little dry. I wanted to be aware of my heart pounding. It gave me the edge I needed to play my best![6]

Although the preceding sources of anxiety are not the only causes of tension for tennis players, they do represent the most prevalent ones. After getting a clearer understanding of what makes you anxious, the next step is to consider how this excess anxiety affects you both physically and mentally.

How Excess Anxiety Is Manifested Physically

In attempting to understand how excess anxiety affects you physically, the best place to start is with the *fight-or-flight response*. This fight-or-flight response takes place as the body prepares itself for a potentially dangerous situation. It has evolved through thousands of generations to protect the human species from imminent harm or danger. It is an automatic protective system, which is extremely effective in keeping you alive. Here is a brief description of how the system works.

The first thing that happens is that you recognize a potentially threatening situation. This signals the body to activate the adrenal glands to release several hormones, including adrenaline, norepinephrine, and cortisone. These hormones are assigned to prepare the mind and body for an emergency situation and to help speed everything up. The heart rate and breathing intensify, and panting allows you to quickly eliminate carbon dioxide. The muscles in your body start to tighten, and it becomes difficult if not impossible to differentiate between muscles that should be relaxed and those that should be tense. Even the muscles surrounding the lungs begin to tighten causing shortness of breath, making breathing more rapid.

This system energizes you during threatening situations and gives you the ability to react quickly to danger. The problem arises, however, when this system is activated because, for example, the upcoming tennis match is stressful or threatening. Tennis requires precision, timing, coordination, and clear thinking, not just brute strength; thus an excess of adrenaline can, and usually does, generate a high level of arousal which makes it extremely difficult to perform with the precision necessary to effectively control your strokes. The following are some of the specific physical problems caused by excess anxiety.

Muscle Tension—Coordination Losses

One of the most obvious and debilitating effects of excess anxiety is muscle tension beyond appropriate levels. To properly stroke a tennis ball requires that certain muscles are contracted while other muscles are relaxed. For example, in hitting a serve, you should be vigorously contracting the extensor muscles in your arm while relaxing the flexor muscles. When you become too anxious and uptight, however, you also start to contract your flexor muscles; this destroys the smooth, rhythmic coordination of the serve. Similarly, if you hit with topspin on your groundstrokes, you need to have a loose wrist to come over the ball. If your forearm and wrist muscles are too tight and tense, this will prevent you from rotating your wrist over the ball. As you hit with less topspin you have less margin for error, which usually means more unforced errors.

Increased muscle tension is accompanied usually by a decrease in blood flow. When you become anxious and nervous, you lose that all-important *feel* that is critical to touch shots. You tend to grip the racquet with the classic death grip, taking most of the finesse out of your game. Without feel you usually lose your rhythm and smooth coordination, which can spell disaster.

Reduced Flexibility

Another result of excess anxiety is reduced flexibility or range of motion. This is usually a result of the increased muscle tension just discussed. To hit with power usually means that a player is using sound mechanics as well as taking the racquet through a full range of motion. When players get tense, however, they contract the wrong muscles (known as antagonists) which limits their flexibility and range of motion.

Take for example the service motion. When you want to hit a big, powerful first serve, you should be bringing your racquet behind your head, dropping the racquet head to the "scratch your back" position. This allows for greater velocity of the racquet head as well as a forceful wrist snap. The problem that arises is that excess muscle tension in your forearm and shoulder muscles can reduce your backswing, thus preventing you from getting your racquet head in the proper position. These muscles need to be relaxed during the preparation of the backswing, but many tennis players tend to contract all of their muscles when trying to hit a hard serve. If you watch John McEnroe serve you will notice that he is very slow, deliberate, and relaxed as he takes his racquet back in preparation for the serve. This allows him the greatest range of motion so that he can generate more velocity and wrist snap on the forward swing.

Another area in which reduced flexibility due to muscle tension can adversely affect your tennis game is in the follow-through. You are well aware of how important it is to follow through on your shots to increase control and power. When you get too tense, however, you tend to start pushing the ball with little or no follow-through at all.

Fatigue

One of the by-products of excess anxiety is that you tend to become more easily fatigued. Contracting a muscle for prolonged periods of time will eventually tire out the muscle, which is what happens when you are tense since we tend to contract inappropriate muscles for extended periods of time. For example, many tennis players get tight in their neck and shoulder muscles; this is a common place where excess tension is manifested. It is not uncommon to see a lot of the top players rolling their heads around in order to reduce tension and fatigue in the shoulder and neck area.

How Excess Anxiety
Is Manifested Psychologically

I have just discussed how high levels of anxiety can negatively affect you from a physiological point of view. Excess anxiety can also have some psychologically detrimental effects including impaired concentration, poor judgment, and mental fatigue.

Reduced Concentration

One of the ways in which too much tension can affect you is by hurting your concentration. Anxiety can distract you and hamper your ability to focus on the point being played. When you are anxious, you are more likely to focus on worries and anxiety rather than the task at hand. Let's take a typical situation in which you have won the first set and are up 5-4 in the second set, serving for the match. As you are on the brink of closing out the match, you start the game by losing the first point and are now down love-15. All of a sudden you begin to get a little anxious and start to think about what might happen if you lose this game. You think about the possibility of losing the set and having to play a third set; and then you might even lose the entire match and everyone will say that you choked. All of these thoughts are distracting and meaningless: they have nothing to do with playing and winning the next four points. Thus, your concentration is broken and you cannot focus on what you have to do to close out the match. Unfortunately, this scenario (and others like it) is typical for many tennis players, which keeps them from playing up to their potential. I will discuss the relationship between anxiety and concentration in much greater depth in chapters 5 and 6.

Impaired Strategy and Tactical Judgment

A second problem area that arises due to increased anxiety concerns strategy and tactics. The typical reaction is that, as your anxiety increases, you tend to start making decisions and judgments that are not consistent with playing percentage tennis. One mistake I have seen in many tennis players as they become more anxious is that they stop playing their game and forget about their game plan. Recall the example given above in which a player is serving for the match. I have often seen players start to select shots that they had not used earlier in the match; that is, a player may have come into the position of serving for the match by serving and volleying on almost every point. After being passed by a great return of serve, however, the player gets nervous about losing the game and decides to stay on the baseline and trade groundstrokes. This usually results in a break of serve because it is not the optimal strategy to win points against this particular opponent.

Anxiety can affect your judgment on not only choosing the proper shot but also deciding how to hit that shot. When the pressure continues to build, I have often seen tennis players either overhit or start to push the ball. Anxiety can cause you to overhit and go for too much because the longer a point goes on, the more anxious you might become. To avoid these feelings of anxiety and tension they go for a low-percentage shot in order to end the point, one way or another. Conversely, they might start to push the ball because they are afraid to hit out and make a mistake. So, they either wind up in a pushing game with their opponents (as in many junior matches where each ball clears the net by 20 feet) or, by pushing with their opponents, they let them take the offensive and come to net to pressure them into a mistake. In either case, their anxiety has produced a strategy that is inconsistent with letting them play up to their potential.

Giving Up—Stop Trying

Anxiety can do more than temporarily wreck your concentration or ruin your tactical judgment. On a more global level, excess anxiety can arrest the development of your skills and affect your overall attitude toward your game. This can occur because anxiety is generally unpleasant, and this typically results in poor performance, leading to more anxiety and frustration. Because it is natural to avoid what is unpleasant, you can develop an aversion to or dislike for tennis in order to avoid further frustration. Or, you might be so anxious about a particular stroke, like your backhand or volley, that you do everything in your power to get around hitting these shots. Of course, if you want to improve a shot, you have to practice it more, not less.

In terms of match performance, excess anxiety can cause you to stop trying and not give 100% effort. This occurs because one way to reduce your anxiety is to get off the court as quickly as possible. To accomplish this, all you have to do is go through the motions, and you can be off the court in no time at all. I have seen players "tank" matches just because the anxiety they were feeling was so disturbing that the best way to relieve the tension was to get off the court. Of course, this is not the proper solution to the problem. I will try to present some other solutions throughout the book. But first, we will take a closer look at the relationship between arousal and tennis performance.

Arousal-Performance Relationship

For many years, coaches across various sports have tried to psych up and pump up their athletes for the big match, game, or traditional rival. Based on extensive research and observation, it is now obvious that the overused approach of the "Win one for the Gipper" speech in the locker room is not necessarily the best way to generate arousal and maximize performance. Strategies for humiliating, degrading, insulting, berating, or, in some fashion, verbally abusing athletes also do not work in most situations. This kind of motivational technique will usually result in the players becoming psyched out instead of psyched up. In fact, this is one of the most important distinctions a tennis player can make. Being psyched out is caused by worry and anxiety which leads to overarousal. You have to learn to reach your optimal level of arousal so that you can perform up to your potential.

Your Optimal Level of Arousal

Research has demonstrated that the relationship between arousal and performance can best be described as an inverted-U curve (also known as the

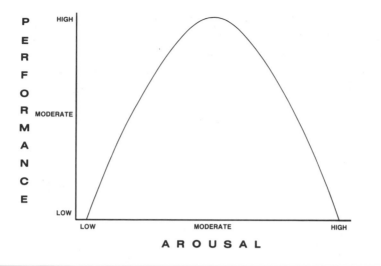

Figure 3.1 Inverted-U Hypothesis

Yerkes-Dodson Law, see Figure 3.1). In its simplest form, performance will increase as arousal increases up to some optimal level, whereupon further increase in arousal will produce a decrease in performance. This means that you perform poorly sometimes because you are underaroused and sometimes because you are overaroused. At the top of the inverted-U curve exists the optimal level of arousal where your performance is maximized. As a tennis player, your goal is to consistently be able to reach your optimal level of arousal for each match and tournament. As you might expect, or have experienced firsthand, this is not so easy to accomplish. That is why one of the major goals of this book is to help each of you reach your optimal level of arousal on a consistent basis.

Individual Differences

It is important to note that the optimal level of arousal differs with each individual. Some people perform best at relatively low levels of arousal whereas others are at their best at relatively high levels of arousal. This can best be seen in Figure 3.2. Players A, B, and C perform best at different levels of arousal, although they all have an inverted-U relationship between arousal and performance. That is why it is important not to compare yourself to other players, because all tennis players function differently. Jimmy Connors may play best when he slaps his leg and verbally exhorts himself, whereas Chris Evert may reach her top performance by taking a deep breath and relaxing. Why this is the case is usually related to our basic personality structure and previous competition experience. Just as

some people are introverts and others extroverts, or some people are morning people while others are night owls, tennis players each have their own
unique way to display and cope with arousal. So do not be concerned with
how others get themselves emotionally ready; rather, just focus on your
own optimal state of arousal. I will discuss how to do this in the next
chapter.

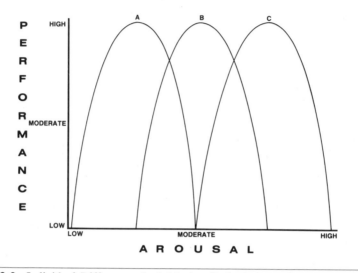

Figure 3.2   Individual Differences in Achieving Optimal Arousal

Underarousal

In your attempt to reach your optimal level of arousal, it has been noted
that you can be either underaroused or overaroused. Let us first look at
the problem of underarousal. In its classic sense, this usually occurs when
you do not take your opposition seriously because you perceive them as
lacking the skills to give you a tough match. You believe that all you have
to do to win is show up for a match because you expect little resistance
from your opponent. So, you might start out lackadaisically, putting forth
a minimum effort and not being at the top of your game. At the same time,
your opponent may sense this opportunity and begin to believe that it might
be possible to win today, thus raising the level of that person's game. As
you quickly fall behind in the match, you realize that the opponent is tougher
than anticipated and you attempt to get your game back on track. Unfortunately, as we probably have all experienced, this is not easy to do. Once
you are down, you try too hard, anxiously attempting to get back in the
match. Your anxiety increases as you fall further behind, and you cannot
believe that you can actually lose this match. Simultaneously, your op-

ponent is becoming more and more confident and is playing better than usual, which makes it especially difficult to come back.

In my work with tennis players this scenario is one that I hear all too often. In fact, when I ask players to list their weaknesses from a mental standpoint, invariably one of the things that surfaces is taking an opponent too lightly and then getting nervous and uptight when they fall behind. Although this does not happen with regularity for most players, it is a particularly discouraging and costly experience, especially if you are serious about your rankings or tournament records. Some suggestions for increasing arousal during the match will be provided at the end of chapter 4.

The other aspect that is usually associated with underarousal is lack of motivation due to boredom, fatigue, or overtraining. This results from hectic travel schedules, conflicting activities, or just too much tennis. This occurs especially in young players who put in a lot of hours on the court and subsequently cannot get pumped up or motivated to play, especially in practice. The constant repetition of hitting against the ball machine or drilling forehands, backhands, serves, and volleys sometimes becomes boring and undermines motivation and desire. This carries over to matches in which the player does not even want to be on the court, which results in a less than all-out effort. Ways to enhance motivation through goal setting will be presented in chapter 11.

Overarousal

Although tennis players experience underarousal at times, the problem affecting most, if not all, players is being too anxious or overaroused. In terms of the inverted-U relationship, you are functioning at a point past your optimal level of arousal which can cause performance problems. At the outset of this chapter, I discussed the sources of excess anxiety for tennis players as well as why and how this can, in turn, produce subpar performance. The individualized nature of the game of tennis, the scoring system (in which each game is a separate entity and thus a 6-0, 5-0 lead does not insure a victory), and the exacting nature of the game make tennis players prime targets for nerves and feelings of apprehension. Various strategies and techniques will be suggested in the next chapter to help you more effectively cope with your anxieties.

Summary

This chapter has provided you with a better understanding of how and why excess anxiety and pressure can affect your performance. The first thing to do is to realize what makes you uptight, as different things upset different people. When pressure gets too high it can result in a variety of physical and mental breakdowns which can disrupt your game and take the fun out of playing. The key thing is to try to find an arousal level that is optimal for you; too little or too much arousal will mentally hurt your performance. This is not easy to do; many players struggle to maintain a balance between being too pumped up and excited and being too lethargic and underaroused. The next chapter will provide you with exercises, techniques, and suggestions to help you reach and maintain your optimal performance state.

 **CHAPTER 4**

Psychological Skill #1: Regulating Anxiety

The previous chapter presented the sources of anxiety, its mental and physical effects, and its relationship to performance. Being able to control your anxiety level is extremely important for achieving your ideal performance state. An important starting point is to develop a keen awareness of your own optimal arousal level.

Self-Awareness of Arousal and Anxiety States

One of the first steps to take in controlling your arousal levels is to become more aware of these feelings during practice and competition. This involves self-monitoring your feeling states and recognizing how these are associated with your performance outcomes. If you are like most of the tennis players I have worked with, you will be able to identify certain feeling states that are associated with top performances and other states that are associated with poor performances. To accomplish this increased awareness of your arousal states, I recommend the following procedures.

First, think back to your best performance, during which you were really in the zone. Try to visualize the actual match as clearly as possible. Also try to focus on what you were feeling and thinking on the court. Do not try to rush yourself; take at least five minutes to relive this special day in your tennis experience. Now, complete the items presented in Table 4.1. In this particular case, because you are reconstructing your best performance, you would circle "1." Moving on to the second item, if you felt moderately anxious, you might circle "4." There are no right or wrong answers; you are doing this to get a better handle on the relationship between your own psychological states and tennis performance. After doing this for your best performance, do the same thing for your worst performance.

Table 4.1   Checklist of Performance States

Played extremely well	1	2	3	4	5	6	7	Played extremely poorly
Extremely relaxed	1	2	3	4	5	6	7	Extremely anxious
Extremely confident	1	2	3	4	5	6	7	Not confident at all
Extremely movitated	1	2	3	4	5	6	7	Not motivated at all
Complete control	1	2	3	4	5	6	7	No control at all
Automatic	1	2	3	4	5	6	7	Constantly thinking
Muscles relaxed	1	2	3	4	5	6	7	Muscles tense
Extremely energetic	1	2	3	4	5	6	7	Extremely fatigued
Positive self-talk	1	2	3	4	5	6	7	Negative self-talk
Extremely enjoyable	1	2	3	4	5	6	7	No fun at all
Focused concentration	1	2	3	4	5	6	7	Unfocused
Effortless	1	2	3	4	5	6	7	Great effort
High energy	1	2	3	4	5	6	7	Low energy

After you have completed this exercise, compare how you responded to the two performances. Most tennis players who tune into their feeling states recognize that their thoughts and feelings are distinctly different when comparing playing well with playing poorly. This is just the beginning of your awareness training. What you should do now is make several blank copies of the checklist (Table 4.1) and monitor your feeling states and performance over the next few weeks in both practice and match situations. Complete the checklist immediately after each outing on the tennis court. Of course, your psychological state will vary from time to time throughout a match. If this is the case, break down your performance into the first set and second set, completing a separate checklist for each one. You might have felt a certain way for the first four games and then differently during the rest of the match, and thus you might complete two cards using this criteria. You are only estimating your feeling states so do not expect absolute precision, which is virtually impossible. If you are diligent about this procedure you will be amazed at how quickly your awareness of your mental states will be enhanced. With this awareness you will have taken a giant step to reaching your optimal level of arousal on a consistent basis. Remember that the most important observation that you can make is to understand the relationship between how you feel on the inside and how you perform on the outside. Your ultimate objective is to gain a high degree of control over your feelings. The exercises and strategies provided in this chapter are designed to accomplish this goal. The exercises are concerned particularly with reducing anxiety and increasing arousal.

Reducing Anxiety

A major objective of chapter 3 was to highlight the fact that excess anxiety can produce inappropriate and increased muscle tension which ultimately leads to performance decrements. When your muscles become too tense your movements will likely appear awkward, jerky, rigid, and uncoordinated. Most top tennis players are quite skillful at detecting very subtle increases in muscular tension and make the necessary adjustments. They can sense that extra tension in the shoulder and neck area, for example, will block the body's natural sense of rhythm and timing when hitting a serve.

A common problem among tennis players, however, is that they tend to tense up all their muscles when trying to hit with more power. In fact, the opposite is true: Hitting or serving a tennis ball harder usually requires relaxing major muscle groups that work against the muscles required to perform a particular movement. To increase power in tennis you need to increase the speed of your racquet head and improve body mechanics. How many times have you consciously tried to hit your serve 100 miles per hour, ending up not hitting it that hard and losing your accuracy in the process? Some recent studies have found that asking athletes to give 80% or 90% effort will improve performance more than requiring 100% or 110% effort. Similarly, just asking athletes to relax their jaws has produced performance improvements. It is important to realize that relaxing your muscles is associated with achieving maximum power and accuracy and that trying to muscle out shots will only result in loss of power and decreased accuracy. The following are some established techniques to induce relaxation.

Progressive Relaxation (Muscle Relaxation)

To control anxiety, probably the most utilized relaxation technique in sports was developed by Dr. Edmund Jacobson.[1] He called it progressive relaxation because you progress from one muscle group to the next until all the major muscle groups are covered. Some of the major tenets of progressive relaxation include the following:

- Tension and relaxation are mutually exclusive. It is not possible to be relaxed and tense at the same time.
- It is possible to learn the difference between tension and lack of tension. Although most people are not aware or sensitive enough to discriminate between small increases or decreases in muscular tension, they can be taught this skill.
- Relaxation of the body through decreased muscular tension will also decrease mental tension and anxiety.
- Progressive relaxation is accomplished by systematically relaxing and contracting all major muscle groups in the body.

General Instructions.   Jacobson's progressive relaxation involves the tensing and relaxing of specific muscles so that you develop an awareness of the difference between tension and relaxation. Specifically, this skill is learned by inducing as much tension as possible in one muscle group, learning to identify what the tension feels like, and then relaxing that muscle completely and feeling the difference. Your attention is focused on the muscle and on becoming sensitive enough to identify tension in any muscle in order to relax that muscle. As you become more skilled in this technique you will be capable of recognizing tension in a specific muscle like the neck and releasing this tension before serving an important point in a match. This is the goal of progressive relaxation.

Although there are many modifications to Jacobson's basic technique, there are certain conditions that must be met. Each approach to progressive relaxation requires that you get into a comfortable position, preferably lying on a mat on the floor with a small pillow under your head. Try to find a relatively quiet, distraction-free area that has a comfortable temperature. Remove or loosen any tight clothing including shoes. Lights should be dimmed but this is not essential. Take off your contacts if you wear them. Your eyes should be closed and you should take a couple of deep breaths. The first few times you perform the exercise it will take you approximately 30 minutes. You will soon be able to reduce this time as you learn to relax more effectively.

As mentioned previously, the final goal is to acquire the ability to completely relax within a short period of time and eventually be able to relax on cue in the midst of a stressful situation. With three or four practice sessions, many of you will be able to achieve relaxation within five to ten minutes. At this point the muscle tension component can be omitted.

Specific Instructions.   In each step you will be asked to first tense a muscle group and then relax it. You need to pay close attention to how it feels to be tense as opposed to relaxed. The tension phase should take approximately five to seven seconds (as will the relaxation phase), but don't distract yourself by paying too much attention to counting. Tense the muscles until you can really feel the tension and then relax them.

Repeat each exercise for each muscle group twice before moving on to the next group. As you become more skilled and aware you can omit the tension phase and just focus on relaxation. You might start by having someone read the directions to you or you might tape them. It is also possible to purchase a progressive relaxation tape.

1. Get as comfortable as possible.
   * Tight clothing should be loosened and your legs should not be crossed.
   * Take a deep breath, let it out slowly, and become as relaxed as possible.
2. Raise your arms and extend them out in front of you.
   * Now make a fist with both hands as tightly as you can.
   * Notice the uncomfortable tension in your hands and fingers.
   * Hold the tension for five seconds, then let the tension out half way and hold for an additional five seconds.
   * Notice the decrease in tension but also concentrate on the tension that is still present.
   * Then let your hands relax completely.
   * Notice how the tension and discomfort drain from your hands and are replaced by sensations of comfort and relaxation.
   * Focus on the contrast between the tension you felt and the relaxation you now feel.

- Concentrate on relaxing your hands completely for 10-15 seconds.

3. Tense your upper arms hard for five seconds.
    - Focus on the feeling of tension.
    - Then let the tension out half way for an additional five seconds.
    - Again, focus on the tension that is still present.
    - Now relax your upper arms completely for 10-15 seconds and focus carefully on the developing relaxation.
    - Let your arms rest limply at your sides.

4. Curl your toes as hard as possible.
    - After five seconds, relax the toes half way and hold the reduced tension for an additional five seconds.
    - Then relax your toes completely and focus on the relaxation spreading into the toes.
    - Continue relaxing your toes for 10-15 seconds.

5. Point your toes away from you and tense your feet and calves.
    - Hold the tension hard for five seconds, let it out half way for an additional five seconds.
    - Relax your feet and calves completely for 10-15 seconds.

6. Extend your legs and raise them approximately six inches above the floor and tense your thigh muscles.
    - Hold the tension for five seconds, let it out half way for an additional five seconds, and then relax your thighs completely.
    - Concentrate on totally relaxing your feet, calves, and thighs for about 30 seconds.

7. Tense your buttocks for five seconds, then let the tension out half way for another five seconds.
    - Finally, relax your buttocks completely and focus on the sensations of heaviness and relaxation.
    - Concentrate on also relaxing the other muscle groups that you have already dealt with.

8. Tense your stomach muscles as hard as possible for five seconds and concentrate on the tension.
    - Then let the tension out half way for an additional five seconds before relaxing your stomach muscles completely.
    - Focus on the spreading relaxation until your stomach muscles are completely relaxed.

9. Press the palms of your hands together and push so as to tense the chest and shoulder muscles.

- Hold the tension for five seconds, then let the tension out half way for an additional five seconds.
- Now relax the muscles completely and concentrate on the relaxation until your muscles are completely loose and relaxed.
- Concentrate also on the muscle groups that have been previously relaxed.

10. Push your shoulders back as far as possible so as to tense your back muscles.

   - Let the tension out half way after five seconds, hold the reduced tension, and focus on it carefully for an additional five seconds.
   - Relax your back and shoulder muscles completely.
   - Focus on the spreading relaxation until they are completely relaxed.

11. While keeping the muscles of your torso, arms, and legs relaxed, tense your neck muscles by bringing your head forward until your chin digs into your chest.

   - Hold for five seconds, release the tension half way for another five seconds, and then relax your neck completely.
   - Allow your head to hang comfortably while you focus on the relaxation developing in your neck muscles.

12. Clench your teeth and notice the tension in the muscles of your jaws.

   - After five seconds, let the tension out half way for five seconds and then relax completely.
   - Let your mouth relax completely with your lips slightly parted and concentrate on totally relaxing these muscles for 10-15 seconds.

13. Tense your tongue by pushing it into the roof of your mouth as hard as possible.

   - Hold for five seconds, then let the tension out half way and hold for an additional five seconds, and then relax your tongue completely.
   - Focus now on completely relaxing the muscles of your neck, jaw, and tongue.

14. With your eyes closed, squint and rotate your eyeballs upward as if you were looking up.

   - Hold the tension for five seconds, then release it half way for an additional five seconds.
   - Then relax your eyes completely.

- Focus on the relaxation developing in your eyes and also concentrate on relaxing your other facial muscles.

15. Wrinkle your forehead and scalp as tightly as possible.
    - Hold the tension for five seconds, and then release half way for another five seconds.
    - Relax your scalp and forehead completely.
    - Focus on the developing feeling of relaxation, and contrasting it with the tension that existed earlier.
    - Concentrate now for about a minute on relaxing all of the muscles of your body.

16. Controlled breathing is one of the most important elements of the relaxation response; it is possible to bring forth a feeling of relaxation by correct breathing.
    - Take a series of short inhalations, about one per second, until the chest is filled.
    - Hold for about five seconds, then exhale slowly for about 10 seconds while thinking to yourself the word *relax* or *calm*.
    - Think about the word as you slowly let out your breath.
    - Repeat the process at least five times, each time striving to deepen the state of relaxation that you're experiencing.

Mental Relaxation Training (Relaxation Response)

You have just completed a relaxation procedure that will help reduce muscle and, consequently, mental tension. There are other relaxation procedures, however, that focus directly on relaxing the mind because this, in turn, will relax the body. Both techniques will produce a relaxed state, each taking a different path to get there.

General Instructions. One of the most popular and scientifically sound relaxation techniques for calming the mind is known as the Relaxation Response. This was popularized by Herbert Benson,[2] a physician at the Harvard Medical School. The Relaxation Response has taken the basic elements of meditation, eliminating its religious significance. Before discussing the actual technique, it should be noted that many athletes have been using forms of meditation as a way of mentally preparing for competition citing that it improved their ability to relax, focus their concentration, and become more energized. The state of mind produced by this technique is characterized by keen awareness, effortlessness, relaxation, spontaneity, and focused attention. What is particularly interesting about this description is that it contains many of the same elements tennis players use to describe their top performance (see chapter 2). The mental state achieved is seemingly ideal for performing up to one's potential.

Specific Instructions.   There are four simple elements that are necessary to achieve the Relaxation Response. These include a quiet environment, comfortable position, mental device, and passive attitude.

A quiet place is necessary, in which external stimulation and distractions are at a minimum. The temperature should be at a comfortable level and you should feel comfortable and at ease in the environment.

Assume a position that is comfortable for you and that you can maintain for a period of time. There is no set position but it should not be lying down in bed; the aim is not to fall asleep.

The mental device is a critical element in the Relaxation Response. This involves focusing your attention on a single thought or word and repeating it over and over. Although Benson suggests using the word *one*, this is not always appropriate for athletes, who sometimes get caught up thinking about being number one; this causes their minds to wander to thoughts about winning. So, make sure you select a word that has no real meaning to you and does not stimulate your thoughts. Some people have successfully used words such as *relax*, *calm*, or *easy*, repeating their particular word in conjunction with breathing out (exhaling). Every time you exhale, you repeat your word.

The final element of the Relaxation Response is a passive attitude. This is also an important part of the process but, at times, a difficult one to achieve. You have to learn to let it happen, allowing those thoughts and images that come into your mind to move through in a passive manner, making no attempt to attend to them. If something comes into your mind, let it go and refocus your attention on your word. Do not worry how many times your mind wanders; continue to refocus your attention on your word.

Because it is a psychological skill, learning the Relaxation Response takes time. It is recommended that you practice about 20 minutes a day; this takes hard work and discipline. In a very real sense, it represents practicing several of the elements inherent to your ideal performance state. Although the Relaxation Response may appear to be easy to accomplish, you will discover how difficult it is to control your mind and focus your attention on one thought or object. But isn't the goal of concentrating during a point to stay focused on the ball and not let your mind wander? Furthermore, between points you must maintain your concentration, not letting irrelevant thoughts enter your mind. The Relaxation Response teaches you to quiet the mind which, in turn, will help you concentrate and will reduce tension in the body. It is also especially useful for prematch preparation because this is a time when you need to relax and focus on the match and your opponent. Remember that the learning process can be slow at times, similar to learning a new shot in tennis. Perseverance will add a new skill to your repertoire and increase your mental toughness on the court.

Breath Control

As you probably noticed, breathing is a key element to the two relaxation procedures presented above. In fact, one of the easiest and most effective ways to control anxiety and tension is through proper breathing. Your pattern of breathing typically is quite different when you are calm and relaxed compared with when you are nervous and anxious. When you are calm, confident, and in control, your breathing is likely to be smooth, deep, and rhythmical. When you are under pressure and tense, your breathing is likely to be short, shallow, and irregular.

One of the most common mistakes is for tennis players, when performing under pressure, to fail to coordinate their breathing with their stroke production. Research has indicated that breathing in and holding your breath increases muscle tension, whereas breathing out decreases muscle tension. Most tennis players have learned to coordinate breathing out with striking the ball, especially in forceful movements like serving. Some players, like Jimmy Connors, are known as ''grunters'' because they appear to grunt after almost every shot. But what Connors is really accomplishing is making sure he breathes out with every stroke. Unfortunately, when the pressure builds at critical points of the match, many tennis players forget this principle and start to hold their breaths while stroking. This causes increased muscle tension and interferes with smooth stroke production.

Practicing Breath Control. Just like other skills, breath control needs to be practiced. A breath control technique that has proved effective with athletes is presented below. Basically, the focus is on breathing from the diaphragm instead of the chest; this produces a greater sense of being stable, centered, and relaxed.

1. Inhale deeply and slowly through your nose and, as you do, notice how your body seems to lift up. Breathe from your stomach and diaphragm and then let the air taken in fill and expand the central and upper chest. This should be done in a very easy, relaxed manner. Your stomach should be pushed fully outward as the breath is taken in. This inhalation process should last approximately five seconds.
2. Exhale slowly through your mouth in a very relaxed manner. You should feel the muscles in your arms and shoulders relax. As you breathe out and relax you should begin to feel centered and well-

anchored to the ground. Your legs should feel relaxed, yet solid and firm. The entire exhalation process should last roughly seven seconds. It's important that the exhalation be done slowly but at a steady rate.

Applying Breath Control.   In a practical sense, breath control can be used effectively on the court during your strokes, between points, and during changeovers.

As previously discussed, learning to breathe out with every hit will make it less likely that you will feel tense and hold your breath while stroking in pressure situations. Of course, this means that you have to practice breathing out on every shot until it occurs automatically regardless of how much pressure you are under.

One of the best ways to maintain your composure and control your anxiety between points is to use the breathing techniques just described. Focusing on your breathing makes it less likely that you will focus your attention on irrelevant cues, like spectators or opponent antics. In fact, deep breathing just prior to serving helps relax the shoulder and neck muscles while allowing you to feel centered, strong, and ready to play the next point. This is particularly critical after playing a tough point that has required a lot of running, causing your breathing to be short and shallow.

Your breathing skills can also come into play during changeovers, when you have 60 to 90 seconds to rest and compose yourself. If you are tiring, struggling, or feeling tense, this is a good opportunity to pull yourself together. Deep breathing can have a calming effect and slow down the body a little so you can focus your energies on what you have to do in the next game. Many tennis players focus on their breathing during changeovers to take a mental break and reenergize themselves for the match.

On-Court Relaxation Tips (Coping With Pressure)

The techniques described above, especially Progressive Relaxation and the Relaxation Response, need to be systematically practiced and worked on at home until they are learned well enough to be integrated into your practices and competitions. There are, however, a number of on-court cues and tips I have found useful and effective in working with tennis players of varying abilities. Remember that, because each person is different, not all of these may work for you. My goal is to provide you with a variety of ideas to cope with pressure, and you need to select those that best fit your own unique skills, abilities, and interests. Many tennis players have told me that just a little simple cue or reminder can have a profound impact on the quality of their playing.

Smile When You Feel Tension Coming On.   A simple and effective cue is to smile when you are becoming uptight and nervous. It is difficult if not impossible to be mad and upset when you are smiling. By smiling, you can take the edge off the particular anxiety-producing situation; it helps you realize that it does not do any good to get uptight and mad. You will realize that tennis is only a game and allow yourself to refocus on playing the next point and forget about the pressure.

Shake Out Hands, Shoulders, and Neck.   If you watch many of the top players in the world, you will probably notice that at critical times in the match they try to relax their muscles by shaking out the tension. The neck and shoulders are two of the places muscle tension is manifested and, therefore, players will roll their heads around and shrug their shoulders to reduce tension in these areas. Others will shake out tension in their arms as swimmers often do just before the start of a race. Slowly stretching tight muscles is another way to loosen up the tension. Of course, if you have mastered progressive relaxation you will have learned to relax your muscles by the cue word *relax*.

Slow Down—Take Time Between Points.   Many of the players I work with report that when the pressure builds up and they are feeling a little frustrated and mad, they start to play too fast. It is as if the anger and pressure were so great that the easiest way to cope with all of this was to hurry and get off the court. Getting off the court quickly is an ineffective way of dealing with your emotions. When players play too fast they lose concentration and become angrier; a vicious cycle begins. I tell the players I work with, when they feel themselves rushing their serves, to walk slowly to the ball farthest away from them, using it for the next service point. This tends to slow down the process. An even more effective way to slow down is to develop a consistent preserve or preservice return routine. This enables you to slow down and keep composed even under great pressure. Your routine will help you to focus on what you have to do. A more detailed description of the development of these routines will be provided in chapter 6.

Use Cue Words.   Some players have found that reminding themselves to relax helps keep the pressure from building up. Using cue words such as *calm*, *relax*, or *easy* reminds you to keep your muscles relaxed and your mind clear and focused. As mentioned previously, you will be better able to achieve your desired state of relaxation if you have practiced your relaxation skills.

Relax and Go for the Lines.   This statement appears illogical at first glance: How can you relax, yet go for the lines? This was a favorite one of the late Harry Hopman, coach of the great Australian Davis Cup teams, featuring players such as Ken Rosewall, John Newcombe, Rod Laver, Fred Stolle, and Tony Roche. This saying highlights the fact that in order to win the big points you need to be relaxed and go for your shots. As players become more skillful, pressure points are not usually won by pushing the ball and playing tentatively. Rather, the successful players manage to raise the level of their games at critical times and points in the match. This is usually accomplished by playing consistently but taking advantage of opportunities to apply pressure to your opponent. If you have a short ball, don't be afraid to hit it deep near the line and come in behind it for the volley. ''Relax and go for the lines'' does not mean to hit low percentage shots and always go for winners. It does mean that you should not be afraid to make a mistake and hit out when the match is on the line. If you hit your shots and lose, so be it. Give your opponent credit for being better that day. Don't lose a match, having to admit to yourself that it was because you played tentatively and choked up on important points.

Focus on One Point at a Time.   Thinking about what might happen or what did happen usually just increases your anxiety. Your concentration needs to be focused only on the point being played. Keeping your mind on the present is a critical skill and will be discussed more fully in chapter 5.

Do Not Set Out Not to Choke.   Tennis players who have had trouble dealing with pressure in the past often focus on not choking in the upcoming match. For example, after a couple of double faults, players say, ''I hope I don't double fault again and choke.'' Or, after they are leading 5-4 and serving for the match they say, ''I hope I don't lose my serve now as I did the last time.'' It is counterproductive to focus on what you don't want to do. Rather, try to focus on what you need to do for each particular shot or game. Putting doubts in your mind will only increase the probability that these doubts will be realized.

Have Fun—Enjoy the Situation.   Common to all tennis players performing at the top of their respective games is a sense of enjoyment and fun. Most top players look forward to and even relish pressure situations instead of fearing them. Particularly in my work with junior players, I have found that enjoyment of the game, regardless of the pressure, is one of the main factors that keeps young players from burning out. This involves keeping winning and losing in perspective and focusing on enjoying the experience without undue concern for the outcome. You can achieve this by focusing on doing your best instead of beating your opponents. If you can give it your best shot and enjoy the game of tennis for what it has to offer, you will probably be playing the game a lot longer as well as a lot better.

Set Up a Good Game Plan and Stick to It.   One of the things that produces anxiety in tennis players is indecisiveness. In any phase of life, making decisions can be a stressful undertaking. The game of tennis is no exception to this principle as the stress of making decisions in a game can wear on your mind. I have found that one way to reduce indecisiveness is to devise a good game plan and stick to it. One of the sources of stress for tennis players is that they do not know how to play an opponent. They often just go into a match without any preconceived notion of what they will do in certain situations. This invariably leads to more decisions, second-guessing yourself, and, ultimately, more stress. For example, a typical decision that can cause stress is when to approach the net, especially against a consistent baseliner. The question that arises during most points is, ''Should I come to net and try to volley or stay back and try to outlast the player from the baseline?'' This constant decision-making process can wear down players mentally, especially if they feel they are making a lot of wrong decisions. A good game plan removes many of these decisions because you will have already made many decisions before the match has even begun.

A good example of a well-conceived game plan occurred in the Wimbledon finals in 1975 involving Jimmy Connors and Arthur Ashe.

With Connors playing at the top of his game nobody gave Arthur Ashe a chance of winning the match. In preparing for the match Ashe and his coaches decided that the best way to beat Connors was to feed him junk. In other words, because Connors thrived on speed and pace, Ashe hit a lot of slices, soft serves, lobs, and other off-speed shots. Arthur Ashe believed in his game plan (even though he preferred to hit big serves and big shots) and carried it out flawlessly to produce a straight set victory.

Not every game plan works out as well as the one just described. In fact, many tennis players give up on their game plan too soon, overreacting to a couple of good shots. For instance, if you feel that your opponent has a relatively weak backhand passing shot you might decide to come to net and attack that backhand at every opportunity. Unfortunately, the first two times you approach the net, your opponent whistles two beautiful backhand passing shots right by you. At this point, many players would abandon their game plan, reasoning that their opponent's backhand wasn't too weak after all. This can be a fatal mistake. If you have a good game plan, then your opponent's backhand will probably break down during the match if you keep it under pressure. But if you don't pressure that backhand, it may never fold because weak strokes are most likely to break under pressure. Of course, there is the possibility that your game plan was ill-advised or that your opponent is having an exceptional day. In this case, a change in game plan might be necessary. But the main point is to have a good game plan in the first place and give it a legitimate chance to work before you alter it. This can really help reduce some of the pressure.

Set Up Stressful Situations in Practice.   A very successful way to prepare yourself for pressure situations is to occasionally practice under stress. As you become more accustomed to playing under these conditions, you will not be as negatively affected by pressure during actual competitions. There are a number of ways to create pressure in practice, and the possibilities are constrained only by your imagination. One coach I know has his players play singles on three courts. The winner of each point moves up from court three to two or two to one while the loser always moves down to court three. When players get to court one they get a point for every point that they win on that court (playing against the coach) and the drill continues until one player wins 10 points on court one. This player is then rewarded in some way by the coach. This type of drill puts the player under some pressure because each point becomes extremely important, as one bad point can drop the player from court one to three. Other drills can be incorporated into the basic drill by setting up specific stressful situations such as serving at 30-40, hitting a second serve at set point, or playing tiebreakers. This allows you to start to develop strategies for handling pressure situations, including choice of shots and style of play, which will maximize your effectiveness. The point is, the more you design your practice conditions to simulate competitive match conditions, the more prepared you will be to deal with the pressures inherent to competition.

Activation Training

Up to this point I have primarily focused on reducing anxiety and increasing the ability to cope with the competitive stress inherent to the game of tennis. There are certainly times, however, when you need to pump yourself up because you are feeling lethargic and underenergized. Before I discuss how to increase your activation of energy level, it is instructive to know the signs of being underactivated. These signs include the following:

- Heavy feeling in legs; no bounce
- Lack of concern about how well you will play
- Mind constantly wandering; easily distracted
- Feeling bored and uninterested
- Moving slowly; poor preparation
- Lack of anticipation or enthusiasm

You need not experience all of these signs to be underactivated. The more signs that you notice, however, the more likely it is that you will need actively to do something to become activated. Although these feelings can appear at any time, they are most likely to occur when you are not physically or mentally prepared to play. This might be due to a number of things such as not resting enough, playing too much, and playing against a significantly weaker opponent, as well as other significant events in your life. The point is, the quicker you can detect these feelings, the quicker you can start to get yourself back on track.

Specific Techniques

Because excess anxiety is usually a greater problem than underactivation, more specific procedures have been developed to cope with anxiety. There are times, however, when you need to get pumped up. Some suggestions for generating more energy and activating your system include the following.

Use Positive Statements.   Repeat things such as *"Get going," "I can do it," "Hang in there,"* and *"Get tough."*

Forceful Movement. A lot of players pump themselves up by slapping their thighs with their hands, contracting and relaxing their muscles, or vigorously jumping up and down. This stimulates blood flow to the muscles and increases the heart rate.

Increase Breathing Rate. Although I suggested that deep diaphragmatic breathing was preferred over chest breathing, in this particular instance the reverse is true. Taking short, quick breaths tends to activate the system and speed up the nervous system.

Act Energized. At times when you feel lethargic, if you act energetically, you can recapture your energy level. For example, move quickly between points, keep your head up and shoulders back, and walk up on your toes. Many times we take cues from our bodies concerning how we feel instead of having our bodies take cues from our minds.

Mood Words. In addition to short statements like those described above, many tennis players use specific words that tend to activate a more energized feeling state. Some examples include *strong*, *forward*, *tough*, *aggressive*, *move*, *quick*, *fast*, and *hard*.

Challenge. Think of this situation as a challenge to overcome. Pride yourself on getting up for all your matches. Make personal pride and determination your trademark.

Summary

This chapter has provided you with a variety of techniques and strategies to help cope with the pressures inherent to competitive tennis. The first step is to become more aware of the things that make you anxious, the specific game situations in which anxiety affects your performance, and the ways in which you react to these anxiety-producing events. A variety of relaxation procedures were presented to help you cope with excess anxiety both on and off the court. Different players feel more comfortable with different techniques; choose what will work best for your own personal situation. But remember, these techniques need to be practiced before applying them to match conditions. Finally, I presented some hints for increasing your energy level and activating yourself in those situations when you find yourself lethargic and not ready to give a good effort.

CHAPTER 5

Concentration Through Proper Attentional Focus

There's no secret to building concentration. It's something you develop the same way you develop other parts of your game. The mistake most club players make is that they don't practice concentration while they're practicing their strokes. If your mind is going to wander during practice, it's going to do the same in a match. When we were all growing up in Australia, we had to work as hard mentally as we did physically in practice. If you weren't alert, you could get a ball hit off the side of your head. What I used to do was to force myself to concentrate more as soon as I'd feel myself getting tired, because that's usually when your concentration starts to fail you. If I'd find myself getting really tired in practice, I'd force myself to work much harder for an extra ten or fifteen minutes, and I always felt as though I got more out of those extra minutes that I did out of the entire practice.[1]

Rod Laver

Very often in a tennis match, you can point to just one game where for a couple of points you lost concentration and didn't do the right thing, and the difference in the match will be right there.[2]

Bjorn Borg

The preceding statements by Bjorn Borg and Rod Laver, two of the greatest players of all time, pinpoint two of the most important aspects of concentration. First, concentration is a psychological skill that can be learned and developed through practice and dedication. Rod Laver described how he worked on concentration during all of his practices. He and his coaches were really aware that if you don't work on developing concentration in practice, you can't automatically turn on your concentration during a competitive match. This is a mistake that many junior and club players make, believing that it's only important to concentrate in the matches. This attitude will cost you some matches because both practical experience and research has demonstrated that we generally play as we practice. The great athletes in different sports are the ones who are the hardest working practice players even though they may also be the most talented players. The old adage "practice makes perfect" should be modified to read "perfect practice makes perfect"; this certainly applies to the practice of concentration. Although Rod Laver talks about working on concentration on the court, there are also things you can do off the court to improve your concentration skills; these will be discussed in chapter 6.

The second important aspect of concentration, underlined by Bjorn Borg's statement, is that the game of tennis is often decided by a small margin which in many cases can be traced back to a lapse in concentration. The scoring in tennis is such that a brief lapse during which your mind wanders can cost you a match. For example, you are easily holding serve whereas your opponent is struggling. Then at 4-4, 30-30 you are serving and have a high putaway forehand volley, but just as you're about to put it away you see out of the corner of your eye that your opponent is moving in the direction of where you intend to hit your volley. At the last instant you change your mind and try to hit behind your opponent, but miss the line by a few inches. You immediately become mad at yourself for taking your eye off the ball, and you proceed to double-fault. With that break of service your opponent gains some added confidence, serves out the set, continues to play well, and beats you in the second set. You're still thinking about that high volley you missed.

In many close tennis matches, the losing player actually wins more points than the winning player. In these situations, there is little skill difference between the two players; rather, one player is able to concentrate better and win the important points. Although concentration is necessary throughout a match, it is particularly crucial at certain critical points. I will discuss ways to improve concentration later but first I need to define concentration.

The Definition of Concentration

It is probably true that people define concentration in several different ways. To provide us with a common reference point, I will use the definition of concentration as found in sport psychology: the ability to focus on the relevant cues in your environment and to maintain that focus for the duration of the athletic contest. A closer look at this definition will show you how to understand concentration in tennis.

The first part of the definition refers to focusing on the important cues in the tennis player's environment. The most obvious, but often overlooked, cue is watching the ball. Although this would appear to be a straightforward and simplistic task, it is often the downfall of many players. Rather than intently watching the ball, most players only focus in its general vicinity. Another relevant cue for tennis players is focusing on the opponent's movements and racquet work before the opponent hits the ball in an attempt to anticipate its speed, direction, and placement. In addition, some players will try to cue themselves before hitting the ball with words like *racquet back*, *follow-through*, *forward*, *easy*, and *strong*. But in reality, the advanced tennis player must pay attention to only a few key things while playing a point, and these will be more thoroughly discussed in the next chapter. Also relevant, however, are the between point cues of thinking about how you will play the next point and deciding on strategy and the type and placement of serve.

Playing tennis is difficult because, although there are only a few key things to pay attention to, there are unfortunately a wide variety of irrelevant cues that compete for our attention. Some examples are crowd noise, antics of the opponent, previously missed shots, eventual score, things that happened the day before, plans for the evening, a bad line call, or anything else the mind can conjure up. As a result, many tennis players constantly battle to keep these irrelevant thoughts and cues from entering their minds in order to be free to focus on the relevant cues discussed above.

One of the keys to Chris Evert's incredible success lies in her consistency: She makes very few unforced errors. This consistency can usually be traced to her uncanny concentration ability. She is able to selectively attend to what is important on the tennis court instead of getting caught up thinking about her personal life, missed shots, bad line calls, and so on. In essence, she gives the tennis match her undivided attention and is hardly, if at all, aware of other things going on around her.

Concentration means maintaining the focus as well: This is the second part of the definition. Selectively attending to the proper cues at a given point in time is not enough; you must also be able to maintain that focus for a potentially long period of time. A tennis match can easily take two or three hours, and one break in concentration can cost you the match. A recent Davis Cup final match between John McEnroe and Mats Wilander took over six hours to complete, severely testing the physical and mental perseverance of these two great players. The adage "fatigue makes cowards of us all" certainly applies to concentration. Along these lines Billie Jean King has often remarked that "the minute you feel yourself getting a little tired, that's when you have to force yourself to concentrate harder." If you recall, the quote by Rod Laver at the beginning of the chapter also supports this point of view. To keep the mind in tow for such a long period of time, especially when the body is fatigued, is sometimes difficult, but the better tennis player usually copes with the situation effectively. This brings us to our next point: Why is it so difficult to maintain our attentional focus throughout a tennis match?

Problems With Maintaining Concentration

I am often asked why it is so hard to sustain concentration throughout a tennis match. In order to respond to this question, you must understand how the mind works and the specific nature of the game of tennis.

In trying to understand how the mind works, researchers have focused on pinpointing the factors that either enhance or detract from a person's attentional state. Why do you attend to certain cues but are distracted by others? In terms of tennis, why does your mind wander when you are on the court to things totally irrelevant to tennis? If tennis is important to you, then you should be able to focus your attention on tennis only when you are on the court. However, we all know that this is easier said than done.

Understanding why the mind has problems focusing on one thing for extended periods of time is a complex process. In simple terms, your attentional focus is, in most situations, dependent on your motivation and the intensity or importance of different events or stimuli in the environment. For example, if you were at home reading a book and you smelled smoke in your home you would most probably forget about the book you were reading (no matter how interesting) and attend to the smoke to determine if your home was on fire. The principle is the same on the tennis court. The more intense the stimuli, the less motivation you need to maintain your concentration whereas the less intense the stimuli, the more motivation you need to sustain your attentional focus.

To apply these concepts to the game of tennis, consider the following example. You are starting a tournament match against an opponent whom you have beaten handily in the past three matches. Because you anticipate an easy match, your motivation is a little low, you even start thinking ahead to your next opponent who is very good. Since your motivation is low, your concentration is inconsistent, and as a result, your opponent (who really is up for the match) gets off to a quick start and leads 4-1. All of a sudden you feel that the match is starting to get away from you and your motivation is heightened. This translates into increased concentration on the match as you forget about your upcoming opponent and focus on getting back into the match by breaking serve. You bring to the tennis court a mind that is always receptive to things other than tennis. It is your job to keep the mind focused on your tennis game and try to disregard other competing thoughts. The interplay between motivation and concentration is described by Rod Laver.

Staying interested in a match is a lot harder than many people think. Throughout my career, I've always had trouble in the early rounds of a tournament mainly because it was hard for me to psychologically get up until I got to the quarters or the semis. What happened a lot of times is that I would fall behind early, maybe even lose the first couple of sets in a five-set match and then begin to concentrate. Still, it wasn't something I could control from the start.[3]

Of course, not many of us can afford to lose the first set or two before we start to concentrate. But it does raise the point that it takes a lot of motivation to concentrate when you do not feel challenged. Thus, a common problem for many players is the inability to perform well against inferior competition. This is because the perceived absence of a challenge results in lapses in concentration.

The second point regarding the difficulty in sustaining concentration throughout a tennis match concerns the specific nature of the game; that is, tennis is essentially a game of starts and stops. Statistics reveal that the average point lasts approximately 8-12 seconds and requires 3-4 strokes. Of course this will vary depending on the level of competition and type of surface (e.g., clay entails longer rallies than grass) but in general, each individual point does not require too much time.

Most of the tennis players I've worked with do not have a problem with concentration during a point, except perhaps during long rallies on slow surfaces. The problem with maintaining concentration usually occurs between points. The time between points is usually between 10 to 30 seconds whereas most points last about 10 seconds. As a consequence, during the course of a 2-hour match, approximately 40 minutes are spent actually playing tennis, while 1 hour and 20 minutes are spent not playing tennis between points. It is this dead time that really taxes our concentration skills because of the numerous distractions competing for our attentional focus (most of which originate from our own thoughts). If you can maintain concentration between points and games then you will be in the proper state of mind for the upcoming point. Suggestions for effectively utilizing these critical times between points will be presented in the next chapter. First we will take a look at the different types of attentional focus and attentional styles.

Types of Concentration (Attentional Focus)

If you are to improve your concentration, it is important to understand first the different types of attentional focus required in the game of tennis. In fact, one of the difficult parts of the game of tennis is that players must constantly change their attentional focus. Basically, attention can be conceived of as varying across two dimensions: *width* and *direction*.

One way in which tennis players need to control their attentional focus is in terms of its width. Specifically, the width of attention can vary from broad to narrow. A broad attentional focus allows a person to perceive several occurrences simultaneously. Tennis players in doubles have to keep track of their partners, the movements of their opponents, and the location of the ball in deciding what type of shot to hit and where to place the shot. A narrow focus of attention is typical of tennis players who attempt to focus exclusively on the ball in preparation for their shot. All irrelevant events or stimuli are eliminated, and attention is directed only to the ball.

Attention can also vary in its direction ranging from internal to external. Internal attentional focus usually means focusing on our own thoughts and feelings such as ''I need to break her serve this game'' or ''I wonder if I should stay back or come to net.'' An external attentional focus would be characterized by focusing outward (e.g., on the tennis ball, movements of the opponent, crowd, etc.). Table 5.1 presents the four different types of concentration that are used by tennis players as well as other kinds of athletes.

Consider for a moment how attentional focus can change during the course of a tennis match. You are getting ready to play an opponent who beat you the last two times you played. An hour before the match you start thinking about a game plan because your last game plan (staying back

Table 5.1   Four Different Types of Attentional Focus

		Direction of Attention	
		External	**Internal**
W i d t h o f A t t e n t i o n	**Broad**	**Broad-External** Used to rapidly assess a situation (e.g., doubles exchange at net)	**Broad-Internal** Used to analyze and plan (e.g., developing a game plan against a tough opponent)
	Narrow	**Narrow-External** Used to focus exclusively on one or two external cues (e.g., watching the ball)	**Narrow-Internal** Used to mentally rehearse an upcoming performance or control an emotional state (e.g., mentally rehearse the tennis serve or focus on taking a deep breath before serving to relax)

on the baseline and outrallying your opponent) was unsuccessful. You decide that you will be more aggressive and approach the net on short balls as well as serving and volleying in certain situations. This requires a *broad-internal* focus. As you get to the court and begin to warm up, you change to a *broad-external* focus by taking in all the important information about the environment such as the speed of the playing surface, wind and sun conditions, your opponent's movement and strokes, crowd, and so on. At the same time, you are focusing on your own strokes, feeling loose, making good contact with the ball, and feeling comfortable with your footwork as well as attending to other kinesthetic cues to hone your strokes: This is a *narrow-internal* attentional focus. As you finish your warm-up and get ready to begin the match, you start to narrow your focus by watching the ball; this *narrow-external* focus gets you tuned into the match. As I will discuss later in the chapter, your attentional focus will continually change throughout the match, and one of the keys to good concentration is the ability to change attentional focus at appropriate times while maintaining a particular focus at other times.

Figure 5.1 Broad-Internal Attentional Focus

Figure 5.2 Broad-External Attentional Focus

Figure 5.3 Narrow-Internal Attentional Focus

Figure 5.4 Narrow-External Attentional Focus

Attentional Problems Due to Inappropriate Focus

When I talk with tennis players I invariably hear that they have problems concentrating throughout a match. A closer inspection of these concentration problems usually reveals that they are caused by inappropriate attentional focus. In essence, your mind is not focusing on the proper cues at a given point in the match and becomes distracted by other events, thoughts, or emotions. Let us take a closer look at a few of the typical problems that tennis players have in attempting to maintain their concentration.

Attending to Too Many Cues

One of the difficult parts to playing high-level tennis is that there are many distractions in the environment that compete for your attentional focus. Players who have a broad-external attentional style are particularly troubled by other things going on around them; they seem to notice everything that is happening in the immediate vicinity of the court.

For example, spectators can present a problem because they represent a potential distraction that you cannot physically eliminate. Spectators can distract you several ways. One problem arises when you know some of the people in the audience, causing you to start thinking about who is in the audience. Because it is natural to want to look good in front of your friends and family, you will probably try to impress them with your shot-making ability. This can sometimes result in going for shots that are beyond your ability. For example, you may try to hit a backhand topspin crosscourt passing shot while on the dead run instead of a more conservative, but less spectacular lob, or you might try to hit aces instead of getting a high percentage of first serves in at 3/4 speed. In essence, you try to play outside of your abilities instead of realizing your limitations and playing high-percentage tennis. It certainly feels great to hit a spectacular winner in front of your friends, but if you try the shot five times and only hit one winner you are not going to win many tennis matches.

Another way that inappropriately focusing on spectators can undermine your game is through trying too hard. I have been told by many tennis players that having their friends and family in the audience causes them to tighten up and try too hard. Because they want to look good in front of their friends, they really start to press and play tentatively. As they start to play poorly and get behind in the match they feel embarrassed, which just causes them to tighten up more initiating a vicious cycle. Of course, some people play better in front of audiences, but for many of us it is a potential distraction; by inappropriately focusing our attention on the crowd we increase the probability of it adversely affecting our performance.

Besides spectators, there are many other potential distractions that can catch your attention and disrupt your concentration. Many players report that they become distracted by things going on around their courts. Unfortunately, in most tournament situations, we do not get to play on isolated courts where there is nothing else going on. Rather, there are usually people walking around near the courts and conversations of some less-than-courteous spectators which intrude on your consciousness. Furthermore, you can be distracted by matches on adjoining courts due to your own curiosity or to arguments that occur between opposing players. At the U.S. Open, players have to deal with airplanes going overhead periodically. The list of potential distractions is endless, and because tennis players have no control over most of these factors, it becomes all that more imperative to effectively cope with them through proper concentration skills. It is extremely important to be able to develop an external-narrow focus of attention when there are numerous distractions. I will present on- and off-court concentration exercises in the next chapter.

Attending to Past Events

A concentration problem that plagues many tennis players is their inability to forget about what happened on previous points. The inappropriate internal focus on past events has been the downfall of many talented players. Let us take a look at a couple of typical examples of how attending to past cues can literally ruin your concentration.

Imagine the following scenario for a moment. You are serving at 4-4, 30-30 in the first set of an obviously tight match. You decide it is a good time to go for an ace and you hit the serve down the middle, right on the line. In disbelief, you hear your opponent (or the linesman if you have one) call the ball out. You question the call, but the call remains. You are so mad that you do not concentrate on the second serve and double fault. Now you are really mad because you feel it should be advantage-in instead of advantage-out. You proceed to make an unforced error and lose your service. Your opponent holds the service and wins the first set. During your first service game of the second set your mind continues to wander back to the bad line call and you have your serve broken again. You finally pull yourself together and hold serve throughout the match but so does your opponent and hence you lose the match 6-4, 6-4. The loss can be traced back to the break in concentration caused by attending to a past event (bad line call).

Now imagine the same situation as above except that at 4-4, 30-30 in the first set, you have an easy put away volley but you go for too much and miss the line by a couple of inches. You can't believe that you missed such an easy shot and your mind continues to replay the flubbed shot over and over again. You are not really mentally prepared to play the next point but you go ahead and serve anyway. Since your mind is not on the current point you lose the point to a careless error. This further angers you and you go on to lose the set. The scenario continues in a similar manner to the above example. Being able to put negative events behind you and wipe them from your consciousness is a critical psychological skill for tennis players. A player needs a narrow-external focus rather than a broad-internal focus at this point in time. I will elaborate on this later on in the chapter.

Attending to Future Events

Besides having problems with attending to past events, many tennis players also have concentration problems concerning attending to future events. Young tennis players, almost without exception, have problems with future-oriented thinking. This is characterized by focusing on the future consequences of certain actions. Some of the typical "what ifs" include:

- What if I lose (win) the next point?
- What if I lose (win) this game?
- What if I lose (win) the first set?
- What if I lose (win) the match?
- What if I lose (win) my service?
- What if I lose my big lead?
- What if I get blown out?
- What if I double fault?
- What if I don't close out the match?

What all of the above statements have in common is their irrelevance to the particular point on which you should be concentrating. It doesn't do any good to think about what will happen if you have your serve broken; this only negatively affects your concentration on winning the next point. Worrying about what might happen acts purely as a distraction and, as suggested in chapter 3, can cause excess muscle tension and tentative playing.

Sometimes the future-oriented thinking has little or nothing at all to do with the particular match or opponent. As mentioned previously, your mind sometimes wanders during a match to things like what you will be doing that evening, what you need to do at school or work the next day, and so on. These thoughts may not even be voluntary; all of a sudden you

find yourself thinking about things that have nothing to do with the match. This can be very frustrating, and matches can drift away from you as your concentration lapses. It is important to stay in the present and keep an external focus on the ball during points and an internal focus on your breathing and strategy between points.

Paralysis By Analysis

Another type of inappropriate attentional focus that can lead to performance problems is focusing on body mechanics during the stroke. It is important to understand when an internal-narrow focus is beneficial and when it is detrimental to performance. Let us take a closer look at this phenomenon.

When you are learning a new stroke or refining your technique on a particular stroke it is important to focus your attention internally to get the kinesthetic feel of the movement. For instance, if you were working on your serve you might want to focus on such things as the transfer of weight, the scratch-your-back position with the racquet, a strong follow-through, and the height of the ball toss (although you probably should try to correct just one thing at a time). If you were changing from a two-handed to one-handed backhand you would need to focus on getting the feel of the new movement because of the natural tendency to revert back to your old habits. Until you integrate this new movement pattern and stroke to the point that they become automatic, your performance is likely to suffer. This is what practice is all about: to focus on improving your strokes by getting a better feel of the movement.

The problem arises when this type of internal-narrow thinking takes place during matches. This usually occurs when you start to have problems with one of your strokes. For instance, let's say that you start missing several backhand passing shots that you normally make. A common way to deal with this problem is to focus more attention on the backhand. You start to monitor how you're hitting your backhand and may ask yourself some of the following questions depending on the types of errors: Am I following through? Am I dropping my wrist? Am I in good position? Am I opening up too soon? Am I keeping my elbow tucked in? Is my backswing too high? Am I hitting the ball too late? As you search for the answer to why your backhand is failing you, you start to attend to the mechanics of your stroke using an internal-narrow focus of attention. This often leads to too much thinking, causing a "paralysis by analysis."

For most advanced tennis players, the pattern of stroke production becomes automatic. This does not mean that no thinking occurs on the tennis court; rather, that too much thinking about stroke mechanics during the match is usually detrimental to performance because the mind gets in the way of the body. The more you tend to analyze the more likely you are to break the natural fluid movements that make for a smooth and efficient tennis stroke. A narrow-external focus on the ball with a minimum of attention paid to body mechanics during rallies will maximize your chances of good performance. Between points and during changeovers may be more appropriate times to focus internally. During the course of a point, where rapid decisions and reactions are paramount, an internal focus on your stroke mechanics will likely overload the system resulting in more errors. During practice is the time to get the feel of the shot and focus on error correction whereas match play should involve a predominantly narrow-external focus of attention.

Choking—An Attentional Problem

One of the worst things that can be said about tennis players is that they "choked." Although there is little agreement among tennis coaches and tennis players on the exact definition of choking, the general consensus is that it usually results in impairment to performance. Take the following situations. You have won the first set 6-2 and are leading the second set 5-3, serving for the match. Your serve gets broken and you go on to lose the second set and the match. Or, in another situation, you split the first two sets and are serving at 4-4, 30-40. As the point progresses you hit a forcing approach shot and your opponent throws up a feeble lob. With all the time in the world to put the ball away you wind up smashing the ball into the net, thus losing the game. Your opponent holds her serve to win the match. In a final situation, you have split sets and are serving for the match at 5-4, 30-30 in the third set. On the next two points you double fault to lose the game but you come back to break your opponent's serve and win the match. In which of the above situations did you choke? If your responses are anything like those I get from tennis coaches and players in my workshops, then there will not be a whole lot of agreement concerning which situations constitute choking. This is because there are no right or wrong answers.

One of the problems with defining choking is that most people focus on the single performance like double faulting, missing an easy overhead, or making an unforced error. However, choking is much more than the actual behavior—it is really a process that eventually leads to impaired performance. Double faulting at match point may or may not be a result of choking. We must understand why the tennis player double faulted. Let us take a closer look at the process that is characteristic of what we have come to call choking.

To begin with, choking usually occurs in a situation that is emotionally important to the player. Thus tennis players playing in big matches where great importance is placed on their success are more prone to choke, especially during critical points in the match. This does not mean that you have to be playing at Wimbledon for a match to be important; playing in the finals at your local club tournament could be really important and stressful to you according to your level of competition.

This increased sense of pressure causes you to tighten your muscles. Your heart rate and breathing start to increase along with other physical changes (see chapter 3). The key breakdown, however, occurs at the attentional level. Instead of focusing externally on the ball and the opponent, your attention becomes more narrow and internal as you start to focus on your own fears and worries of losing and failing. At the same time, the increased pressure reduces the flexibility in your attentional focus, and you have problems changing your focus as the situation dictates. This inappropriate attentional focus coupled with excess anxiety causes a variety of performance problems such as impaired timing and coordination, fatigue, muscle tension, rushing shots, and poor judgment and decision making. Thus, the double fault, unforced error, blown overhead, and missed volley are just the end result of inappropriate attentional focus brought about by excess pressure. The choking process is displayed in Table 5.2.

Table 5.2 The Process of Choking

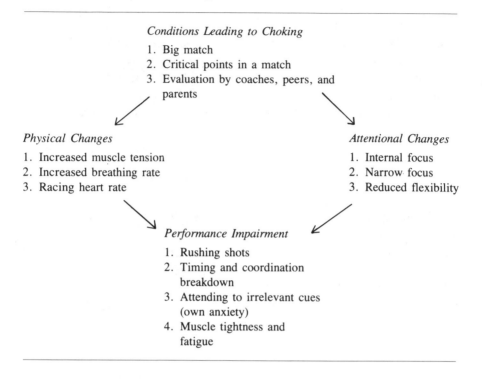

Conditions Leading to Choking

1. Big match
2. Critical points in a match
3. Evaluation by coaches, peers, and parents

Physical Changes

1. Increased muscle tension
2. Increased breathing rate
3. Racing heart rate

Attentional Changes

1. Internal focus
2. Narrow focus
3. Reduced flexibility

Performance Impairment

1. Rushing shots
2. Timing and coordination breakdown
3. Attending to irrelevant cues (own anxiety)
4. Muscle tightness and fatigue

Summary

This chapter has discussed how proper concentration is related to having the appropriate focus of attention. Concentrating over a long period of time such as in a tennis match can be extremely difficult especially due to the stop and start nature of the game. Some common problems were discussed such as attending to future or past events and thinking too much causing a paralysis by analysis. Finally, the concept of choking was presented indicating that it resulted from an interaction of excess anxiety and inappropriate attentional focus. The next chapter will provide some techniques and strategies to help improve your concentration and focus on the proper attentional cues.

CHAPTER 6

Psychological Skill #2: Improving Concentration

I have just discussed several attentional problems in tennis that can wreak havoc with a player's game and ability to concentrate. If we are going to improve our concentration ability, we need to take a systematic approach to practicing better attentional control.

On-Court Tips to Improve Concentration

Once again, different players react differently, so I have provided a number of strategies, techniques, and on-court exercises. Choose the ones that seem to work best for your personality and playing style.

Practice Eye Control

One of the problems many players run into is becoming distracted by sights and sounds around the court. This is usually a problem between points when you are not actively involved in the match per se and your mind has a greater tendency to wander. I have seen many players who, with eyes darting around the court, become distracted by the opponent's antics, spectators, players on adjacent courts, or any of a number of other distractions. One good way to keep your eyes from wandering is to focus on your strings between points. This will prevent your eyes from looking around and focusing on other irrelevant and competing cues. Several players such as Jimmy Connors and Ivan Lendl pick at their strings and keep their heads down, focusing on their racquets until they are ready to begin the point. The key is to pick something that can maintain your focus of attention and prevent your eyes from picking up distractions. Roy Emerson, the great Australian champion, states:

> It starts the minute you walk out on the court. When I'd go out for an important match, I'd look straight down at the ground, as if I were looking for a dime on the court. I never looked at the ballboys or the umpire, or even my opponent. I never even listened to anything. All I heard was noise.[1]

Focus on the Seams of the Ball

This idea comes from the work of Tim Gallwey[2] in his book *Inner Game of Tennis*. This fundamental focus is often overlooked, even by top players who sometimes have problems watching the ball. You often hear the same refrain from players at all levels: "Watch the ball." Experiments have been conducted demonstrating that many tennis players focus on the general vicinity of the ball but do not actually maintain focus on the ball itself. Not watching the ball becomes more of a problem as a point gets longer and as a match gets longer because of fatigue. Also, when your opponent is hitting hard serves and crisp volleys and groundstrokes it becomes even more critical that you keep your eyes on the ball.

Watching the seams of the ball usually produces some interesting results. First, many players realize that they see the ball better if they focus on the seams. Looking for the pattern made by the seams causes us to start watching the ball from the moment it leaves our opponent's racquet to the time it hits ours. Since there is a tendency to start watching the ball earlier, players often report that the ball even begins to appear bigger or to be moving slower.

Another benefit of watching the seams is that the mind becomes so absorbed in watching the pattern that it forgets to think about all the distracting things that interrupt concentration. The mind is less likely to wander to irrelevant thoughts. This usually will result in a more fluid, natural, and rhythmic stroke production.

Although many players find the practice of watching the seams immediately helpful, it takes a while to be able to stay completely focused on the seams. Because the mind's tendency is to wander this must be practiced a great deal before it can be effectively and consistently employed in match competition. Besides focusing on the seams, you might try concentrating on the trajectories of each shot, both yours and your opponent's. Notice the height of the ball as it passes over the net, its speed, and whether it is rising or falling as you make contact with your racquet. This makes you more aware of the rhythm of the alternating shots of each point, and helps your mind stay focused on the point.

Play One Point at a Time—Disregard Future and Past

The importance of playing one point at a time cannot be overemphasized. For example, in an interview, Bjorn Borg was asked: ''What was the most important reason for your incredibly successful tennis career?'' Although Borg obviously was gifted with the outstanding physical attributes of quickness, speed, and timing, he responded by saying that ''*It was my ability to play one point at a time and not worry and think about what just happened or what might happen. The only thing that was important was the point about to be played.*''[3] Not many people know that Borg had to learn this skill when he was a junior; he had a reputation of blowing up and letting things get to him. In fact, he got so bad that his parents put his racquet in the closet for six months and forbid him to play tennis. If he wanted to play he was going to have to learn not to let things bother him and just concentrate on one point at a time.

Because the mind is so open to incoming messages it's sometimes hard to stay focused on the present. Remember that playing one point at a time is one of the characteristics that tennis players note when describing their peak performances. Staying in the present requires a focused concentration between points; this is when our minds tend to drift to future and past events. The next chapter on self-talk will provide some practical suggestions for staying in the present.

Practice With Distractions Present

One of the things that throws off our concentration is being distracted by noise, movement, or other disruptions. It always amazes me how a small sound made by someone in the crowd or a little movement can destroy totally a player's concentration. Basketball players are able to stand at the foul line and shoot free throws while potentially hostile spectators yell, wave their hands, and stomp their feet. But if someone moves in the stands or talks loudly during a tennis match, most tennis players become distracted and upset. For example, many players have commented that they are distracted by planes flying over the U. S. Open, which is in the flight-path of La Guardia Airport.

One of the ways to better cope with the potential distractions in a tennis match is to prepare for these events in advance. This can be accomplished by systematically practicing with some of the things that typically distract you and break down your concentration. Many basketball coaches, for instance, will pipe in loud crowd noises to get the players used to playing and shooting in that environment. Tennis players can train in the same manner to better prepare themselves for match competition. You (or your coach) might arrange to have some people stand around the court and talk or walk by your court from time to time. In addition, if you have problems concentrating in windy conditions or serving into the sun you must make it a point to practice under these conditions. Because these situations are aversive to many players, they avoid them in practice and then are totally psyched out if these circumstances arise in a match. Do not always practice under ideal conditions. The more practice you have dealing with potential distractions and other aversive conditions the better prepared you will be to effectively cope with these during matches and block them out. Here is how Jimmy Connors blocked out the heat and humidity during a match.

It was hot out there—really hot—but I knew that if I started thinking too much about the sun, I wouldn't do my best. I didn't worry about it while I was on the court, but when I was sitting down, with the sun beating down, it started to get to me a little. So I just blocked it out, and pretended it wasn't there. That's what you have to do in tennis— not let yourself think about anything that can have a negative effect on your game.[4]

Use Cue Words

One of the best ways to keep your mind focused on the match is through the use of cue words. These are simply words that you can use to help trigger a particular response. These cue words can have an instructional component (e.g., *racquet back, follow through, firm wrist*) or they can be more motivational or emotional (e.g., *move, strong, quick, relax, easy*). The key is to keep the cue word simple and let it trigger the desired response. In returning serve, if you are being caught flat-footed hitting off your back foot you might use the cue word *forward* to get you moving into the ball. In hitting the volley you might use the trigger *firm* or *punch* to emphasize hitting out in front of you; if you are not getting full extension of your arm in hitting overheads you might use the cue *reach* or *stretch*.

A cue needs to be meaningful to you and helpful for focusing attention on the specific response that will produce successful results. It is particularly useful when learning a new stroke or variation of a stroke or when trying to break a bad habit. Also, if you're tuned in to your body and sense that you are not concentrating on a certain aspect of your game, then cue yourself on that aspect. Rod Laver provides an example of being attentive to the importance of his movement and footwork.

If I can get my feet moving, then everything falls into place a little better for me. Usually when a player isn't concentrating well, it will show up in one or two technical areas, like not watching the ball or not getting the shoulders turned. So rather than simply telling yourself to concentrate, the thing to do is to focus on that one thing that's giving you trouble.[5]

The number of different cues you can use is endless. Some additional examples will be provided shortly in the discussion of self-talk and concentration.

Nonjudgmental Thinking

One of the biggest obstacles to maintaining your concentration during a match (or practice) is when you evaluate your shots, seeing some shots as good and others as bad. Basically, you are assigning a positive or negative value to an event. You like it when you ace your opponent but are disgusted when you miss an easy overhead. These judgments are your personal, ego reactions to how you view your tennis game.

This process of evaluating your shots can only hurt your performance. After judging a couple of shots as bad, you will tend to start generalizing. This usually results in judgmental thoughts such as "I always miss the easy ones," "I have a terrible serve," or "I'm just a choke artist."

As Tim Gallwey has noted, these kinds of thoughts and judgments lead to impaired performance and strokes begin to lose their rhythm, timing, and smoothness. Your brain starts to override your body and this results in trying too hard, tightening your muscles, and playing tentatively. You need to look at your performance in a nonjudgmental way. This does not mean you should ignore errors but you should see your shots as they are without adding anything to them. For example, you observe in a match that your first serve percentage is 40%. This observation does not include labeling your serve as terrible, which usually leads to anger, frustration, and discouragement. Instead of evaluating, you notice that most of your faults are going into the net rather than being hit long. This is a cue either that your ball toss is too low or that you are rushing your serve. In response, you alter your ball toss or service motion to correct the problem. Thus, merely observing what is happening and using that information in a positive manner can translate into not only better performance but a more enjoyable experience.

Do Not Change Your Mind On a Shot

As mentioned earlier, tennis is a game of decisions, many of which have to be made in less than a second. This puts a lot of pressure on a player to make good decisions and play the percentages. Many players, however, complicate the decision process by making two or three decisions on one shot. This type of thinking is usually detrimental to your concentration; one of the fatal mistakes you can make is attempting to change your mind on the type or placement of your shot at the last moment. Let's use the example of hitting a backhand passing shot. Your opponent has hit a fairly good deep approach shot, and you instantly decide to pass down the line. As you take your racquet back, however, in the corner of your eye you see that your opponent is coming down the line; at the last instant you try to go crosscourt but hit the ball into the net. In another situation, you have a pretty easy overhead and your opponent is just standing still on the backhand side, seemingly giving up the point. As you get ready to hit the ball into the open court you notice your opponent dashing across the court to that very spot. You try to change your shot and hit behind your opponent but the ball goes wide.

In both situations, changing your shot at the last moment produced an error. It is extremely difficult, even for very experienced players, to change the shot selection and produce a winning shot. This is because you have to make several minute but critical adjustments instantaneously in timing, angle of the racquet, and footwork. The mistake that players make is watching their opponents instead of watching the ball. As you get set to hit a shot you need to focus only on the ball and hit that shot crisply. If you execute the shot well, you will probably win the point even if your opponent has outguessed you. For example, if your overhead is strong, the best your opponent can do is throw up another lob; you will still be in control of the point. Or, if your passing shot down the line is low and hard, your opponent probably will not be able to put it away, giving you another chance for a pass. If you are at the net with a "sitter," you can wait for your opponent to commit and then hit to the open court. In almost all situations, make up your mind, believe in your decision, and execute the shot to the best of your ability.

Routines to Improve Concentration

Another way to minimize distractions and focus concentration is to develop a consistent routine. Because tennis is such a fast sport, the best times for routines to be developed occur when there is a break in the action. Therefore, I have tried to develop some routines for service and service return.

Service Routine

Of all the shots you hit in tennis, the serve is the only one that is under your complete control. Every other shot is a response to your opponent's shot. Consequently, this is a perfect opportunity to develop a service routine that will stand up under the stress of competitive pressure. With consistent practice, a routine will eventually become a habitual, automatic, and natural part of your serve. It will also provide a rhythm and a sense of comfort that will not desert you even under situations of intense pressure.

If you watch top players with excellent serves like Martina Navratilova, John McEnroe, Ivan Lendl, Pam Shriver, Boris Becker, and Stefan Edberg you will notice that their routines and timing remain the same throughout the match. This is because they have planned, practiced, and perfected their routines so that they can feel comfortable throughout the match. The routine reduces anxiety and narrows concentration on the critical aspects of the serve. The following are some suggestions for a service routine; it is important to note that you should develop a routine with which you are comfortable; that is, one that fits your needs, abilities, and personality.

1. Determine Positioning and Foot Placement. For most players a routine should begin by placing the toe of the left foot (right foot for lefthanders) a certain distance behind the baseline. The exact distance is not as important as keeping that distance consistent. For example, if you move into the ball by moving the front foot, you might stand farther back to avoid a foot fault. Also you need to determine your positioning along the baseline for serving into the ad and deuce courts and whether this changes for doubles. John McEnroe, for instance, stays far away from the center line especially in serving to the deuce court, which is somewhat unusual. The important point is to determine your optimal position based on your service skills, and maintain that position. A final suggestion is to be aware of the distance between your feet and the angle at which your toes are pointing. This placement is critical because it controls the rotation of the body and the way the weight is transferred.

2. Decide on Service Type and Placement. I am constantly amazed by the decision process (or, more appropriately, the lack of it) of tennis players concerning service. When I ask: "Why did you choose to hit a slice serve wide to the forehand side on the deuce court?" I often get the response "I felt like it" or "It just seemed like the right serve at the time." A server needs to be much more systematic concerning choice and placement of the serve. Some questions you should be asking yourself include:

- What is your best serve?
- What has been working for you lately?
- What will your opponent be expecting?
- What is the highest percentage serve?
- What is the specific situation in the match?
- Are more errors being produced on the forehand or backhand side?

Although this may seem like a lot to think about, some of the decisions can be made before the match if you know your own and your opponent's strengths and weaknesses. In addition, as you become more experienced, you can assimilate all this information in a short period of time. It is important not to overlook the importance of your choice of serves. A good server does not necessarily overpower the opponent; rather, a good server keeps the opponent guessing and off balance. It is sometimes informative as well as enlightening to chart what types of serves lead to winning points and service return errors. Maximize your service ability by making high percentage decisions on service type and placement.

3. Adjust Racquet Grip and Ball.   After deciding on the type of serve, you should check and adjust your grip. Different serves may require slight adjustments in your grip; the racquet needs to feel comfortable in your hand. In addition, you need to place the tennis ball in your hand. Although many people are taught to serve with two balls in their hands, I recommend always serving (in both practice and competition) with only one. First, if you serve with two balls in your hand, you must master two different tosses, one for the first serve and one for the second. Second, by holding only one ball in your hand you are forced to take the next ball out of your pocket after a fault. This will inevitably slow you down and cause you to take a little more time before hitting your second serve. Many players have a tendency to rush their second serve, particularly under pressure; it is therefore important to follow the same deliberate routine regardless of the situation.

4. Take a Deep Breath.   A deep breath to relax the neck, shoulders, arms, and wrist is a good way to settle yourself down just before you serve. After a long point, many players start to serve before they have fully recovered. You might need two or three deep breaths and you should not start your service motion until you are calm and psychologically ready to start the point.

5. Bounce the Ball for Rhythm.   Most tennis players will bounce the ball a set number of times before serving to help their rhythm. It does not really matter how many times; the object is to feel comfortable. After bouncing the ball it is a good idea to take another deep breath to further relax before you start your service motion.

6. See and Feel the Perfect Serve.   Just before you begin your service motion, try to see and feel yourself hitting the serve into the exact spot that you decided upon. This will help program your muscles and give you confidence that you can indeed hit the serve the way you want to. Chapter 8 will explain in great detail the technique of imagining yourself hitting certain shots.

7. Focus On Ball Toss and Serve to Programmed Spot. You are now ready to toss the ball, which is a critical part of successful serving. You might find it helpful to pick a spot (generally above and in front of you) where you want to toss the ball. Focus your attention on this spot and then just let your serve run off automatically.

Right now, you might be saying that you can't be thinking about all these things when you serve, and in part, you are absolutely correct. You must practice your routine until it is virtually automatic, requiring a minimum of conscious thought. You know you will have accomplished this goal if you consistently go through your routine on all your serves, regardless of the situation. Remember also that these are just suggestions, and in the final analysis you need to feel comfortable with whatever routine you decide is best for you.

Service Return Routine

Returning serve is potentially a very stressful and unpredictable position to be in; you need to react swiftly and accurately to your opponent's serve. You must be aware of the changes in the server's racquet position or angle; react to the speed, spin, and placement of the ball; and decide on the type and placement of your service return. This must be done within a matter of a couple of seconds or less.

Many players fall apart when returning serve because they allow themselves to become nervous, mentally distracted, or intimidated. This can result in a stroke that is different from and less efficient than your normal return. Your mind-set and mental preparation are critical to have a successful and consistent service return. For some players, playing against a serve and volley player helps their service return (as opposed to playing against a baseliner) because against serve and volley players they really concentrate and try to keep the ball low when returning serve. Conversely, for other players, returning against a net rusher intimidates them causing them to push or overhit their returns. In either case, your mind-set prior to returning serve can have a large impact on the way you perform. Some suggestions for a service return routine are presented below.

1. Decide on Where and How to Return the Serve. Tennis players often make the mistake in returning serve of not deciding in advance what they want to do with the serve. It is important to decide whether you are going down the line, crosscourt, down the middle, deep, or short. You must also know whether you will chip and charge, use topspin, slice, or lob. Being confused as to how to return serve as the server goes into the service motion is a terrible feeling. In this situation, you probably will not hit a good solid return. Of course, if the server is really tough, it may be all you can manage to simply get the ball over the net. Most often matches are won and lost, however, by making consistently good returns off returnable serves. For example, if the server stays back, try to keep the ball deep; if the server comes to net, try to keep the ball low so the server has to volley up. Most second serves, regardless of the level of play, are returnable, and good decisions on how to return these serves will reduce unforced errors.

2. Take a Deep Breath and Take Your Ready Position. After deciding on how you want to return serve, take one or two deep breaths to relax and get into your ready position. Be sure you are physically and mentally ready before you assume the ready position. If you are having trouble returning serves, change your position; this also gives the server something to think about. For example, if you are having trouble with your backhand return, move over and dare your opponent to hit to your forehand. This may be enough to throw off the server's rhythm.

3. Picture the Desired Service Return. As in the service routine, picture hitting the perfect service return. See yourself making contact out in front of you and hitting the ball to the desired spot on the court.

4. Focus On the Server and Ball Toss. Now is the time to focus all your attention on the server and ball toss. Most servers will provide you with subtle cues concerning the type and placement of their serves. For example, many servers toss the ball a little further away from the body when attempting a wide slice serve and more directly overhead when hitting an American twist serve. Careful attention to the ball may give you a little edge on what to expect.

5. Use Cue Words. In preparing to return serve it is useful to use a cue word that reminds you to do a certain thing or execute a certain movement. For example, repeating the word *forward* will help you remember to step into the return and stay up on your toes. Keep your cues simple and personally meaningful.

Exercises to Improve Concentration: On-Court

Besides the various things you can do during a match to help focus your concentration, there are a couple of specific drills you can work on during your practice sessions to improve your attentional focus.

Exercise 1

This exercise can be accomplished by use of a ball machine or someone feeding from a basket of balls. Fill the ball machine (or basket) with balls of two colors (e.g., white and yellow) and place the machine on the opposite baseline. Designate one color ball as *down the line* and the other color as *cross court*. It is then your job to watch the ball closely, determine its color, and then hit it down the line or across the court. This will force you to really focus on the ball so you can determine its color early and then perform your appropriate response. To increase difficulty, move the ball machine up to the service line and then halfway between the service line and the net. This puts increased pressure on you to really watch the ball, make quick decisions, and then hit crisp down-the-line or cross-court passing shots.

Exercise 2

To keep your mind in the present and prevent it from wandering, try this drill. Use a ball machine that has a fair range of velocities. Stand at the net in volley position and then have someone set the machine at a comfortable speed. Gradually increase the velocity, and you should see that you become more and more concentrated. As balls start to rocket at you at high speed there is no time left for your mind to wander and become distracted. Some players, as the balls continue to get faster, start to become fearful and tighten up their muscles. If you have this tendency, take a deep breath, focus on the seams of the ball, and try to hit the ball in front of you. This exercise should make you more aware of what it feels like to be totally focused on the present.

Exercise 3

This next drill is designed to improve concentration, steadiness, patience, and discipline. Depending on your skill level choose a specific number of groundstrokes that you would like to hit without making a mistake (e.g., 20, 40, 50, 80, 100). Have someone feed you balls or hit against a ball machine and try to reach your goal. If you miss, you have to go back to zero; the pressure should start to build as you approach your goal. You can increase the difficulty by requiring that the ball be placed in a certain part of the court. For example, to improve your depth, you might try to hit shots between the service line and baseline; to work on placement, you can limit your shots to down the line or crosscourt. The variations are limitless, and the end result will be more focused concentration and mental discipline.

Exercise 4

The next exercise will help your decision-making ability concerning when to approach the net. Make a line approximately three feet behind the service line on your side of the court. Whenever your partner's shot lands between the line and the net you must start moving to the ball before it bounces (early judgment and decision are imperative) and then try to take the ball early and approach net. Your partner then has the option for either a passing shot or a lob.

Exercises to Improve Concentration: Off-Court

I have just presented a variety of exercises that can help improve your concentration on the court. If you are really interested in working on your concentration skills, then you should also work on improving them off the court. A number of exercises are provided to help you refine these skills which will allow you to better focus your attention and maintain that focus over time.

Exercise 1

One technique that has been used extensively to increase concentration is known as the *grid* exercise. This requires a block grid with each of the blocks containing a two-digit number ranging from 00 to 99 (see Table 6.1). The object is to scan the grid and within a given period of time (usually one minute) put a slash through as many consecutive numbers as possible, starting with "00". The same grid can be used several times by just starting with a higher number than in your previous attempt (e.g., 22, 37, 44, etc.). In addition new grids can be made using any combination of numbers. It has been reported that athletes who have the ability to really concentrate, scan, and store relevant cues will usually score in the upper 20's and into the 30's in terms of the numbers they find in sequence in one minute. This exercise has been used extensively in Eastern Europe as a precompetition screening device. It really can give you a sense of your concentration at a given point in time.

Besides helping you learn to focus your attention and scan the environment for relevant cues (e.g., in doubles), the exercise also has the advantage of creating different situations. For example, you can add distractions such as music or people talking to you, and you can do it where there is noise or any other potential distractions to your attention. As your

Table 6.1   Concentration Grid Exercise

42	32	39	34	99	19	64	44	03	77
97	37	92	18	90	53	04	72	51	65
40	95	33	86	45	81	67	13	59	58
78	69	57	68	87	05	79	15	28	36
26	09	62	89	91	47	52	61	64	29
00	60	75	02	22	08	74	17	16	12
25	76	48	71	70	83	06	49	41	07
31	10	98	96	11	63	56	66	50	24
20	01	54	46	82	14	38	23	73	94
43	88	85	30	21	27	80	93	35	55

concentration improves you will be better able to block out the distractions and focus exclusively on the task. And isn't this what you want to accomplish in your tennis game—complete absorption and the elimination of all potential distractions.

Exercise 2

The first exercise worked on your ability to pick out relevant cues and scan your environment quickly and effectively. This next exercise helps you focus your attention and maintain that focus. Begin by finding a quiet place where there are no distractions. Get a tennis ball and place it in your hand getting a good sense of how it feels: its texture, color and any other distinguishing characteristics. Put the ball down and try to focus your attention on it. Try to examine it in great detail. If your thoughts wander, bring your attention back to the ball.

Chart how long you can maintain your focus on the ball. You will find out that it's not that easy to stay focused on one object, but that is what you need to do in a tennis match. If you can increase your ability to focus on the ball, this will help your concentration. Practice this exercise regularly.

When you can maintain concentration for five minutes without being distracted, practice with distractions (e.g., noise, people talking, music, T.V., etc.). Chart how long you can maintain your focus of attention despite these distractions. These are the kinds of things your mind will have to deal with when out on the tennis court.

Exercise 3

An exercise to improve concentration and minimize distractions prior to a match involves seeing yourself playing the match in your head. This is described by ex-tennis professional Ron Holmberg.

I'm pretty sure I went a lot further than most players in getting myself mentally prepared. I used to actually sit down before a match and picture in my mind every possible shot sequence I could imagine that might take place in the match. I'd imagine a short ball coming to my forehand and I'd picture myself actually making the approach shot and then putting away the volley. I'd imagine myself hitting a drop shot and picture myself moving up to the net to hit a drop shot my opponent hit. In this way, I was able to get my mind into the match even before I stepped onto the court. [6]

Holmberg's description supports mental rehearsal to help concentration. This will be discussed in more detail (chapter 8) and is an excellent way to prepare for a match (chapter 12).

Exercise 4

This is a fun exercise which demonstrates how mental concentration influences your muscle reactions. It requires a string about 10 inches long, to which a small weight such as a ring or key is attached, making it into a small plumb line. Stabilize the elbow of your dominant hand on a table while holding the string between your thumb and forefinger. Now raise your hand and forearm to a 45 degree angle lifting the string and attached object off the table. Start concentrating on moving the weight in a certain direction (e.g., clockwise, counterclockwise). You will probably notice that the weight begins to move in the desired pattern just by thinking about it. This highlights the fact that your thoughts have a direct relationship to your muscular responses; controlling your thoughts and focusing your attention properly is critical to your tennis success.

Summary

This chapter has provided you with a variety of on-court and off-court tips and exercises for improving concentration. Many players feel that concentrating means trying harder. In reality, concentration is a skill that must be developed through a systematic program of exercises. Once again, similar to coping with anxiety, although a variety of techniques and strategies are presented, you must choose what feels most comfortable to you. This requires you to identify what your weak areas are in terms of concentration and focus on improving them with the appropriate exercises.

CHAPTER 7

Psychological Skill #3: Self-Talk

A common theme in the discussion of attentional problems revolves around the idea of self-talk. Although I have alluded to the importance of self-talk, its critical position in relation to concentration warrants special attention. Thus, this chapter will be devoted to understanding the nature of self-talk, the problems with self-talk, and some ways for effectively coping with self-talk.

Types of Self-Talk

All of us who play tennis talk to ourselves with some degree of regularity. Of course, the frequency and content will vary from person to person and from situation to situation. Anytime you think about something you are in a sense talking to yourself. Self-talk becomes an asset when it enhances self-esteem, attentional focus, and performance. Self-talk that helps a tennis player to stay appropriately focused in the present, not dwelling on past mistakes or projecting too far into the future is known as *positive self-talk*. Conversely, self-talk that gets in the way because it is inappropriate, irrational, counterproductive, or anxiety-producing is called *negative self-talk*.

Before I discuss how self-talk works and how specific types of self-talk can be used in different situations to improve performance, it should be noted that, when performing at their best, many tennis players report that they had no thoughts at all (see chapter 2). In fact, many sport scientists and practitioners have stressed that peak performance does not occur when athletes are thinking about the skill. Rather, they emphasize that elite performers turn performance over to an unconscious or automatic level that is free from the interference of thought.

Although it may be desirable to strive for such thought-free performance, most tennis players do think before, during, and after matches as well as practices. For example, Bjorn Borg has described tournament tennis as several hours of thinking, thinking on every point. These thoughts can have a profound impact on a player's concentration, not to mention self-esteem, self-confidence, and anxiety. Therefore, it is important for tennis players and coaches to control these thoughts as much as possible. As you shall see, it is not thinking itself that leads to performance problems, but inappropriate or misguided thinking. The question should not be whether to think, but how, what, and when to think. Understanding how self-talk works will help you to answer these questions.

How Self-Talk Works

We are not disturbed by things, but rather the view we take of them.
Epictitus

There is nothing either good or bad, but thinking makes it so.
Shakespeare

The above quotes sum up the critical role that our thoughts have on our emotional responses to events. However, most of us probably feel that events themselves determine our emotional and physical responses. Take the following example. You are playing in the finals of an important tournament that you have never won before. You win a tough first set 7-5 and are serving for the match at 5-4 in the second set. Your serve is broken, however, due in part to your tentative play and in part to your opponent's tough service returns. You proceed to lose the second set and then lose the match in a 7-6 tiebreaker in the third set after being up 4-1. After the match you are discouraged, mad, and upset with yourself for blowing the match and are so depressed that you don't even want to practice next week. You think to yourself: "Why should I continue to work hard when I obviously can't win the big match?"

Now consider yourself in the same situation except that your reactions to this adversity are different. Instead of putting yourself down you objectively look at the match and say to yourself, "I realize that I lost my concentration and I need to work on this part of my game if I expect to win the championship next time." In essence, you realize you have the ability to win but just need to work a little harder in practice.

This simple illustration highlights the idea that events in and of themselves do not cause your emotional reactions such as depression, anger, anxiety, hopelessness, and frustration. Rather, it is how you interpret the event that determines your response. The relationship between an event, your self-talk, and your response is displayed in Table 7.1. As the figure demonstrates, self-talk plays a pivotal role in a tennis player's reaction to situations (especially adversity) and directly affects future actions and feelings.

Table 7.1 Process of Self-Talk

Event (Environmental Stimulation)	Self-Talk (Perception/Evaluation)	Response (Emotional, Physiological, Behavioral)
Unhealthy Examples		
Flunking an exam	"I'll *never* pass this course or finish college"	Discouragement, depression
Missing an important shot during a tennis match	"What an idiot I am—I'll never win now"	Anger, hopelessness, increased muscle tension
Healthy Examples		
Flunking an exam	"I know what to study for now—I'll do better"	Optimism, motivation to do better, calmness
Missing an important shot during a tennis match	"Keep your eye on the ball—this match isn't over"	Better concentration, optimism, calmness

Ways to Use Self-Talk

Although positive self-talk is crucial for good concentration, the uses of self-talk extend into several areas of tennis. The following is a brief discussion of the many ways that self-talk can help tennis players.

Self-Talk for Skill Acquisition

As you become more proficient in tennis, the nature of your self-talk should invariably change. For example, if you are just learning a new stroke like the backhand, self-instructional talk is usually useful to remind yourself of certain key aspects of the stroke. Simple cue words like *wrist firm, reach,* or *elbow straight* can help in learning the appropriate sequence of action. Even at the beginning level, however, self-talk should be kept to a minimum; ororverbalization can cause the paralysis by analysis discussed earlier. As your backhand improves, your self-talk should become shorter, less frequent, and more focused on strategies than technique cues. Your goal is to reduce conscious control and strive for more automatic action; the use of a cue like *smooth* might help achieve this state. In addition, your self-talk should focus more on what you are trying to achieve rather than on the mechanics of the stroke. Before serving, for instance, think of where you want to hit the serve rather than how to hit it. When hitting a volley, however, there is usually no time for thinking, and you have to respond automatically to the ball.

Self-Talk for Breaking Bad Habits

Many tennis players are forced to cope with changing bad habits. Trying to switch from a two-handed to one-handed backhand, from slice to topspin on the backhand, or from an eastern to western forehand grip all make severe demands on our concentration. These changes are extremely difficult because we must unlearn an automatic response and learn a new response. Self-talk can be an effective tool to help break the bad habit and program the new one.

In changing a stroke or breaking a bad habit you (and a coach or pro if you have one available) need to decide on the most relevant and appropriate self-instructional cue or cues that will help make the new response automatic. The greater the change the more self-instruction will be necessary. In addition, it is important to focus on what to do rather than what not to do. Telling yourself, "don't drop your racquet head" gives no information about what to do; it only highlights the negative. You should always work on telling yourself what to do such as "Follow through" or "Keep the wrist firm" as this reinforces the habit you are trying to make automatic.

Self-Talk to Initiate Action

Self-talk can also serve to get you started or motivated. It has been shown that runners have increased their speed by using words such as *quick* or *fast*. Footwork in tennis might be enhanced with similar words, especially if we are feeling slow and lethargic. Hitting aggressive volleys might be triggered by cue words such as *strong, crisp,* or *forward*, whereas a serve might be cued by words such as *smooth, reach,* or *explode*. Besides cueing particular strokes, self-talk can serve to motivate us by such cues as *wake up, get going, move, pick it up* and *get tough*. We tend to respond quickly to these types of commands from coaches, and these same commands coming from ourselves can work just as well.

Self-Talk to Sustain Effort

Although getting started is sometimes hard, once you get into the match you need to work hard to maintain a high degree of effort. This can be difficult when fatigue starts to set in during a long match. Of course good conditioning is essential, but effort can also be sustained through self-talk. Phrases such as *hang in there, stay with it, keep it up,* and *hold onto it* can help maintain effort when the body is starting to fatigue.

Techniques to Improve Self-Talk

The first step to gain some control over your self-talk is to become more aware of what you say to yourself. Unfortunately, most of us are not really in touch with our self-talk and many times do not even realize the powerful impact it can have on our performance. Carefully reviewing the way in which you use self-talk can help you identify beneficial and detrimental kinds of self-talk and the circumstances or match situations associated with positive and negative self-talk. The important point is to learn how and when to talk to yourself. Two ways to get a better understanding of the relationship between self-talk and your tennis performance are through retrospection and self-monitoring.

Retrospection

One good way to get started is to try to remember your self-talk during previous matches. I have found that it is usually instructive to try and remember some of your best and worst recent performances. As you do this, attempt to identify and record the content and frequency of your self-talk. Most tennis players can identify their self-talk and usually notice a distinct difference between these two situations. Specifically, good performances are usually characterized by positive and instructional self-talk, whereas bad performances are usually accompanied by negative self-talk.

Self-Monitoring

Although remembering past performances is useful, a more accurate way to stay in touch with the nature of your self-talk is through keeping a daily log or diary. You should try to transcribe your self-talk as soon after you get off the court as possible, whether it be after practice or a match. Self-talk that occurs during practice is usually a good indicator of what will occur in matches. In monitoring your self-talk try to be particularly aware of the types of situations or events that trigger negative, self-destructive self-talk which impairs your performance. Some events that typically trigger negative self-talk include the following:

- Missing on every shot
- Losing a big point
- Blowing a lead
- Double-faulting
- Losing serve
- Making unforced errors

Monitoring your self-talk and its effect on performance will undoubtedly open your eyes to the critical role it plays in your tennis game. Once you get a handle on what situations and circumstances produce negative self-talk you will have taken an important step toward winning the mental game.

Although monitoring your self-talk is the first important step you need to take to improve your self-talk, this alone will not necessarily improve your self-talk. Once you become aware of the link between your thoughts and performance, you need to start using this information effectively.

Thought Stopping

One way to cope with negative thoughts is to try to stop them before they hurt your performance. Getting rid of negative thoughts helps you regain the proper focus of attention to the task at hand. Learning the skill of thought stopping involves concentrating on the undesired thought briefly, then using a cue or trigger to stop the thought and clear your mind. The trigger can be a simple word like *stop* or a trigger like snapping your fingers or hitting your hand against your thigh. Each of you needs to decide what is the most effective and natural cue that works for you.

Thought stopping requires a high level of motivation and a focused awareness of your thought-producing process. This is not an easy task because breaking the bad habit of negative self-talk may be as difficult as breaking the bad habit of taking your racquet back too high on your backswing. In my work with tennis players, I have found that it is not unusual to have 30 or 40 negative thoughts throughout the course of a practice or match. Eliminating these usually takes some time and effort; do not expect overnight success.

When first attempting thought stopping, it is best to restrict it to practice situations. Whenever you start thinking a negative thought just say *stop* out loud (or whatever cue you choose) and then refocus on a task-related cue. This will indicate to you (and your coach) that you are working on your new skill. After you start to master this you should just try to say *stop* to yourself. Moving from an external cue to command *stop* to an internalized one such as thinking *stop* in your head may take some time to accomplish.

If there is one particular situation that produces negative self-talk, such as missing an easy shot, you might want to concentrate on that one aspect. This will allow you to stay more focused and be more aware of this particular problem. If you overcome this problem, then move to another area of concern.

Another way to practice your thought stopping is to use imagery (imagery will be fully explained in chapter 8). Close your eyes and imagine the specific situation in which you have been troubled by negative self-talk. Once you have visualized the situation and subsequent negative self-talk, attempt to use your cue to interrupt these thoughts. This should be done many times to habitualize the process. After doing it in your mind and in practice you should be ready to try your thought stopping in actual matches. Old habits die slowly, so keep working on your technique and don't be discouraged if you occasionally fall back on your old habits.

Changing Negative Self-Talk to Positive Self-Talk

Although it would be nice to eliminate all our negative self-talk, in fact, most of us still allow negative thoughts to enter our minds. When this happens, one way to effectively cope is to change these negative thoughts into positive self-talk, which redirects attentional focus and provides encouragement and motivation.

Probably the best way to change negative to positive self-talk is to make a list of all the types of self-talk that hurt your performance. If you have kept a good log, this will serve as a reminder of the situation and accompanying negative self-talk. The goal here is to recognize which situations produce negative self-talk and why. Then, try to substitute a positive statement for the negative one. When this is accomplished make up a table with your negative self-talk on one side and your positive self-talk on the other side. Table 7.2 provides an illustration of what such a table would look like.

Table 7.2   Negative and Positive Self-Talk

Negative Self-Talk	(change to)	Positive Self-Talk
You idiot—how could you miss such an easy shot?		Everyone makes mistakes—just concentrate on the next point.
What will everyone think if I lose?		Just give it your best. Winning and losing will take care of itself.
I hope I don't choke again.		Relax and just watch the ball.
He robbed me on the line call—the ball was definitely in.		There's nothing I can do about it. If I play well I'll win anyhow.
I'll take it easy today and workout hard tomorrow.		If I work hard today then the next workout will be easier.
That was a terrible serve.		Just slow down and keep your rhythm and timing.
I'll never win this match.		Just take one point at a time.
I never play well in the wind.		It's windy on both sides of the court. This just requires extra concentration.

When practicing changing your self-talk from negative to positive the same guidelines apply as in using thought stopping. Specifically, try it in practice first and also imagine using it before attempting it in a match. In addition, because most negative thoughts occur under stress, you should first try to stop the negative thought and then take a deep breath. As you exhale, try to relax and repeat the appropriate positive statement.

Countering Irrational Beliefs

Changing your negative self-talk to positive self-talk will probably not be totally effective if you still believe in the negative statements. For example, if you really believe that your opponent's bad line calls cost you the match, then telling yourself it doesn't matter probably won't help your performance much. Usually at the core of the majority of negative self-talk are what Albert Ellis[2] calls *irrational beliefs*. Such thinking is counterproductive since it negatively affects one's self-confidence, motivation, self-concept, and performance. In my work with tennis players, I have seen examples of a host of irrational beliefs. There are several beliefs, however, that are given consistently by tennis players of all levels when describing their play. These inevitably lead to performance problems; a list of these beliefs is provided below along with suggestions of how to counter them.

1. *I can play perfect tennis.* This belief leads only to a great deal of frustration and disappointment. You can't play perfect tennis, and thinking you can only raises your expectations unrealistically every time you step onto the court. When you think you should be playing perfect tennis, you become tighter physically and begin to press harder. This deteriorates your performance. A more realistic view would be to accept that everybody makes mistakes and to learn from those mistakes.

2. *External circumstances are responsible for my losing.* Those who operate under this belief are losers and poor sports. People who believe this blame everything around them for their losing (the wind, bad spots on the court, etc.). When you lose on the court (just as when you win), you are responsible and you should believe that winning and losing are under your control.

3. *Because I played poorly early in a match, I will continue to play poorly.* This is a common belief held by those who try to predict future performance when there is no reason to. The fact of the matter is, you can never know how well you are going to play on a given day, so don't try to predict it. Sometimes, you can play horribly in the first set of a match and play great the rest of the way. If you let poor performance at the start of a match get you down, it is unlikely that your performance will get any better later. You need to believe that you still can play well despite a poor start.

4. *My performance on the tennis court reflects my worth as a person.* It is not unusual to hear this coming from tennis players. You feel great about yourself on the days you play well, and you feel like jumping off the nearest building on days when you play poorly. Even on the bad days, try to keep in mind that you are still a worthwhile person. If you separate performance from self-worth, your self-esteem can remain fairly stable even when your tennis performance fluctuates. If you don't, you may be on an emotional

rollercoaster ride. You should believe that your self-worth is independent of what you do on the tennis court.

5. *I should get angry and upset every time things don't go the way I want them to on the tennis court.* This belief occurs often when players get overly upset at the slightest problem and seem to let everything bother them. Something goes wrong in every tennis match. What tends to separate winners from losers is the ability to cope with things when they don't go smoothly. Great players are those who can handle missing easy shots and bad calls without letting it bother them during the rest of the match.

6. *I can't learn anything or improve as a result of losing a match.* I find that this particular statement arises when tennis players don't take the time to learn from the matches they lose. Instead, they go sulking off trying to forget the whole thing. It may be that you learn the most when you lose, not win, a match (there are exceptions to this, of course). Smart players try to rethink lost and won matches so that they can glean from them those things they can use in playing the next match.

7. *Being critical of myself before, during, or after a match helps my performance on the court.* Although it may sound like splitting hairs, being self-critical, as opposed to self-evaluative and task-oriented, probably hurts your performance. There is a big difference between saying, "You missed that easy volley, what an idiot you are," and saying, "You missed that easy volley—next time, get your racquet back earlier." If you make a mistake, think about it in terms of how to correct it. Don't harshly criticize yourself, because it only leads to playing worse.

Summary

This chapter has highlighted the critical role that self-talk plays in winning the mental game. It noted different types of self-talk along with the different ways that self-talk is used including acquiring skills, breaking bad habits, initiating action, and sustaining effort. Like other psychological skills, an awareness of how and when you use self-talk is the first step to initiating change. After this is accomplished there are several ways to improve self-talk including thought stopping, changing negative to positive self-talk, and countering irrational beliefs. Self-talk can help reduce anxiety, improve concentration, and, if used correctly, build confidence. Spend some time working on this skill.

CHAPTER 8

Psychological Skill #4: Imagery

Before I play a match I try to carefully rehearse in my mind what is likely to happen and how I will react in certain situations. I visualize myself playing typical points based on my opponent's style of play. I see myself hitting crisp deep shots from the baseline and coming to net if I get a weak return. This helps me prepare mentally for a match and I feel like I've already played the match before I even walk out on the court.

Chris Evert

The above comments represent Chris Evert's testimonial to her belief that rehearsing the match and shots in her mind helps her performance. She is not alone in her belief; many other tennis players such as Arthur Ashe, Billie Jean King, Martina Navratilova, Tim Gullickson, and Tom Gullickson are proponents of the use of mental rehearsal. In addition, testimonials of many elite athletes in a variety of sports, such as Dwight Stones (track and field), Greg Louganis (diving), Jean Claude Killy (skiing), Bruce Jenner (decathlon), O. J. Simpson (football), and Jack Nicklaus (golf) provide additional support for the use of mental rehearsal to help improve performance. Jack Nicklaus, who recently won the Masters at age 45, is particularly detailed in describing his use of imagery before every shot.

First, I see the ball where I want it to finish, nice and white and sitting up high on the bright green grass. Then I see the ball going there;

its path and trajectory and even its behavior on landing. The next scene shows me making the kind of swing that will turn the previous image into reality.[1]

This chapter could be filled with testimonials of athletes regarding their use of mental rehearsal. Although some athletes have been using imagery for a long time, it is only recently that coaches and researchers have started to understand its potential for improving sport performance. We are slowly starting to realize that mental rehearsal should be included in our daily training regimen if we are interested in reaching our potential. Of course, as we will discover, different players will utilize mental rehearsal in different ways, but you should include some form of it in your practice and match play. This chapter deals with imagery, specifically, (a) what it is, (b) how it works, (c) what are its uses, and (d) how to set up an imagery training program.

What Is Imagery?

You have probably heard a variety of terms to describe an athlete's mental preparation for competition. These include mental rehearsal, imagery, visualization, psychocybernetics, and mental practice. No matter what you call it, these techniques all refer to recreating or creating an experience in the mind.

You recreate experiences in your mind all the time through the use of images. Have you ever watched a top player and then tried to copy a certain aspect of that person's game, like the service motion or the way to hit a groundstroke? Or, have you ever tried to remember a time when you played really well and hit the ball effortlessly and then tried to recreate that feeling and stroke production in your mind? We are all able to accomplish this because our mind can remember these events and create a picture of them.

In a similar manner, your mind can create or picture new events that have not occurred yet. For example, in forming a strategy against an upcoming opponent, you might create certain points in your mind and see how you would react to these situations although you never have played this particular person. Your mind can create a situation and thus better prepare you to effectively deal with it.

A common misconception, however, is that imagery only refers to picturing or seeing yourself performing an activity. This is only partially correct since imagery can, and should, involve as many senses as possible. Although imagery is often called visualization, in sport, auditory, tactile, olfactory, and kinesthetic senses are all potentially important.

Let's look at how a tennis player can use a variety of senses. First of all you obviously use your *visual* sense to watch the ball and the movement of your opponent. You employ your *kinesthetic* sense (awareness of one's body as it moves in different positions) to sense where your racquet head is during your backswing or to transfer your weight at the proper time. You can use your *auditory* sense to hear how the ball comes off the strings. The importance of hearing was highlighted several years ago when the "spaghetti racquet" was introduced which involved a different type of stringing. It was soon prohibited; many top professionals commented that it threw off their timing because the ball sounded totally different coming off their opponent's racquet. Although you may not realize it, you rely heavily on auditory information provided by the racquet striking the ball; this tells you about the speed, trajectory, and spin of the ball. You can also use your *tactile* sense to feel how the racquet feels in your hand.

In addition to using your different senses during imagery, it is also important to experience your emotions and feelings. Recreating emotions such as anxiety, anger, joy, or pain through imagery can help control these states.

How Imagery Works

How does just thinking about hitting a perfect serve or playing out points actually help you perform these skills more effectively in an upcoming match? Fortunately, research in this area provides some scientific evidence as to why imagery can be such a powerful tool in enhancing performance. Specifically, two explanations have been put forth.

The first explanation revolves around the fact that vivid imagined events produce an innervation in your muscles that is similar to that produced by physically performing the movement. That is, your brain is incapable of distinguishing between something that actually happens and something that is vividly imagined. In research with Olympic downhill skiers, Richard Suinn[2] monitored the electrical activity in their leg muscles as they imagined skiing the course. Results indicated that the muscular activity in the skiers' leg muscles changed as they imagined skiing down the slope. Muscle activity was highest at certain times and these corresponded to points when the skiers were imagining themselves skiing rough sections in the course which would actually require greater muscular activity. This is in agreement with other studies which have found that imagining a movement produces muscular activity in the appropriate muscles.

When you vividly imagine yourself performing a movement, you use similar neural pathways to those used in the actual performance of the movement. The muscular and neural activity is not as great as when you actually perform the skill, but through imagery you can help strengthen the neural pathways for that skill.

Let's take the example of trying to perfect your serve. Your aim is, typically, to make your service motion more natural and fluid and thereby achieve consistent, fast, and accurate serves. To do this, you take a basket of balls and practice your service motion and swing continually, trying to make your serve automatic (i.e., groove your serve). What you are really doing is strengthening the neural pathways that control the muscles related to serving. One way to strengthen these neural pathways is by imagining that you are executing what you would consider a perfect serve. Through imagery, you can make your body believe that you are actually practicing the serve. You are, in effect, programming your muscles and preparing your body to perform through imagery. The benefits and advantages can be tremendous.

A second explanation concerning how imagery works suggests that imagery can also help athletes understand the movements themselves. One way in which you learn skills is to become more familiar with what needs to be done to successfully perform these skills. You form a mental blueprint for successfully completing the movement. For example, in doubles you need to be familiar with how your partners move along with their strengths and weaknesses to help you decide on the most effective shots and positioning. Another way to use imagery is in planning for a match: You need to think through the best way to defeat your opponent and plan an appropriate strategy. Imagining what you are going to do in your doubles or singles match helps to familiarize you with what will most likely occur and to prepare you to make the correct decisions and responses.

In either case, both explanations for the effectiveness of imagery point to the fact that it can help program you both physically and mentally. The end result will make our tennis strokes more fluid and automatic physically, while at the same time helping you to make the correct decision mentally.

Uses of Imagery

Tennis players can employ imagery in a variety of ways and situations to improve both physical and psychological skills. These will be briefly outlined below.

Control Emotional Responses

One of the areas that troubles many tennis players is letting their emotions such as anger and anxiety get the best of them on the court. Through the use of imagery, you can visualize situations that have caused problems in the past like choking on a critical point or becoming angry at line calls. This time, however, picture yourself dealing with these events in a positive way (using the techniques described in other chapters), such as taking a deep breath and focusing on your breathing when you see yourself becoming too uptight or nervous.

Improve Concentration

Imagery can also enhance your concentration, especially prior to a match. By visualizing the match and your strokes prior to playing a match you prevent your mind from wandering and thinking about irrelevant things. Also, you can imagine yourself in situations where you generally lose your concentration (e.g., after missing an easy shot or getting a bad line call). In this situation, image that you maintain your composure and refocus your attention on the next point.

Practice Strategy

As highlighted by the quote from Chris Evert, imagery can help you set up your prematch game plan. Practicing what you want to do before you get on the court will help you make better decisions during the game.

Building Confidence

Imagery can be used to build self-confidence in your shots. For example, imagining yourself hitting hard, accurate serves gives you confidence even though you might have had trouble with your serve in recent matches. In addition, picture yourself in situations that have destroyed or broken your confidence (e.g., having your serve broken or missing a couple of easy shots) and then imagine that you bounce back with a service break of your own.

Coping With Pain and Injury

A potential use of imagery that is often overlooked is coping with pain and injury. One of the hardest things for a tennis player to go through is sitting out for an extended period of time due to injury. Instead of feeling sorry for yourself you can imagine hitting all your shots, playing matches, and working on drills. There are stories of several athletes who have utilized imagery during periods of inactivity and have come back to achieve their former skill level in a short period of time.

Besides injury, imagery can also help you deal with pain and fatigue on the court. On a very hot and humid day, visualizing yourself in a cool environment (i.e., swimming at the beach) can help focus your attention away from the discomfort caused by the hot weather.

Practicing Strokes

Probably the most well-known use of imagery is to practice a particular stroke or shot. If you are learning a new variation to a stroke such as an American twist serve or topspin backhand or if you are having trouble with a particular shot, imagery can be a valuable tool to help you improve them. The use of imagery is not limited to problem areas in your strokes; it is also helpful for further refining and automatizing your shot.

Error Correction

Imagery can also be used to look back at previous performances and determine when, why, and how certain errors occurred. Much can be learned from your previous performances, especially in terms of understanding why you made certain decisions. Replaying a match in your mind can help you pinpoint your mistakes and take appropriate measures to correct them. Of course, videotapes are also instructive in this regard.

Types of Imagery

When athletes use imagery, they usually image from either an internal or an external perspective. The type of perspective you image from has an important impact on the effectiveness of your image. Thus a brief discussion of these two perspectives will be presented.

External Imagery

One way in which you can image is by watching yourself as if you were in the movies. Or, imagine that you are watching yourself on videotape; external imagery generates the same type of picture. For example, if you image hitting a serve from an external perspective, you would see not only your ready position, toss, swing, and follow-through but also your back and the back of your head because you are taking the perspective of a spectator.

Internal Imagery

As opposed to external imagery, internal imagery refers to imagining the execution of a skill from your own eyes. In this case, you see only what you would ordinarily see when executing this particular skill. It would look as if you had a camera on your head which took pictures of all the things you would see during execution of the skill. Looking at the tennis serve again, you would see your opponent, the racquet and ball in your hands during ready position, the ball toss, and the contact of the ball, but you would not see the back of your head, backswing, or anything else out of your normal range of vision.

Imagery Evaluation

Having been introduced to imagery and its potential uses, you can now begin to consider starting an imagery training program. The first step in

Table 8.1   Sport Imagery Questionnaire

As you complete this questionnaire (adapted from sport psychologist Rainer Martens[3]), remember that imagery involves more than just seeing something in your mind. Vivid images include not only visualizing but experiencing all the senses— seeing, hearing, feeling, tasting, and smelling. Along with these sensations you may also experience emotions, moods, or certain states of mind.

Below you will read descriptions of four general sport situations. You are to imagine the general situation and provide as much detail from your imagination as possible to make the image as real as you can. Then you will be asked to rate your imagery on four dimensions:

1. How vividly you saw or visualized the image
2. How clearly you heard the sounds
3. How vividly you felt your body movements (kinesthetic sense) during the activity
4. How clearly you were aware of your state of mind or felt the emotions of the situation

After you read each general description, think of a specific example of it (e.g., the skill, the people involved, the place, the time). Next, close your eyes and take a few deep breaths to become as relaxed as you can. Put aside all other thoughts for a moment. Keep your eyes closed for about one minute as you try to imagine the situation as vividly as you can.

Use your imagery skills to develop a vivid and clear image of the general described situation. Your accurate appraisal of your images will help you to determine which exercises you will want to emphasize in the basic training exercises.

After you have imagined the described situation, please rate the four dimensions of imagery by circling the number that best describes the image you had.

1 = no image present
2 = not clear or vivid, but a recognizable image
3 = moderately clear and vivid image
4 = clear and vivid image
5 = extremely clear and vivid image

Practicing Alone

Select one specific skill such as hitting a forehand, backhand, serve, or volley. Now imagine yourself performing this shot at the place where you normally practice without anyone else present. Close your eyes for about one minute and try to see yourself at this place, hear the sounds, feel your body perform the movement, and be aware of your state of mind or mood.

a. Rate how well you saw yourself doing this activity.   1   2   3   4   5
b. Rate how well you heard the sounds of doing the activity.   1   2   3   4   5
c. Rate how well you felt yourself making the movements.   1   2   3   4   5

(Cont.)

Table 8.1 Cont.

d. Rate how well you were aware of your
   mood.   1   2   3   4   5

Practicing With Others

You are doing the same activity but now you are practicing the skill with your coach and your teammates present. This time, however, you make a mistake that everyone notices. Close your eyes for about one minute to imagine making the error and the situation immediately afterward as vividly as you can.

a. Rate how well you saw yourself in this
   situation.   1   2   3   4   5

b. Rate how well you heard the sounds in
   this situation.   1   2   3   4   5

c. Rate how well you felt yourself making
   the movements.   1   2   3   4   5

d. Rate how well you felt the emotions of
   this situation.   1   2   3   4   5

Watching a Teammate

Think of a teammate or acquaintance performing a specific shot unsuccessfully in a match such as missing an easy volley or double faulting.

Close your eyes for about one minute to imagine as vividly and realistically as possible watching your teammate performing this activity unsuccessfully in a critical part of the contest.

a. Rate how well you saw your teammate in
   this situation.   1   2   3   4   5

b. Rate how well you heard the sounds in
   this situation.   1   2   3   4   5

c. Rate how well you felt *your own* physical
   presence or movement in this situation. 1   2   3   4   5

d. Rate how well *you* felt the emotions of
   this situation.   1   2   3   4   5

Playing in a Contest

Imagine yourself performing in a match, but imagine yourself playing very skillfully and the spectators and teammates showing their appreciation. Now close your eyes for about one minute and imagine this situation as vividly as possible.

a. Rate how well you saw yourself in this
   situation.   1   2   3   4   5

b. Rate how well you heard the sounds in
   this situation.   1   2   3   4   5

c. Rate how well you felt yourself making
   the movements.   1   2   3   4   5

(Cont.)

Table 8.1 Cont.

d. Rate how well you felt the emotions of   1   2   3   4   5
    the situation.

Scoring

Now, let's determine your imagery scores and see what they mean. First, sum the ratings for your four answers to part "a" in each section, your four answers to part "b" in each section, and so on, recording them in the proper place below.

					Total Score
Dimension					
a. Visual	_____ +	_____ +	_____ +	_____ =	_____
b. Auditory	_____ +	_____ +	_____ +	_____ =	_____
c. Kinesthetic	_____ +	_____ +	_____ +	_____ =	_____
d. Mood	_____ +	_____ +	_____ +	_____ =	_____

If you had all 5's on a given dimension your top score would be 20 with your lowest score being 4. The closer you came to 20 on each dimension the more skilled you are in that particular area. Lower scores mean you need to work on those aspects of your imagery.

this direction is to evaluate your current imagery skill level. I have emphasized the fact that imagery, like all psychological techniques, is a skill that needs to be learned through practice. Some of you will probably be pretty good at it, especially if you have had some prior experience using imagery, whereas others of you may not even be able to get an image in your minds.

To evaluate your imagery skill level, we will use a test developed by Martens[3] that measures how well you can use all your senses while imaging. Follow the instructions and do the best you can. There are no right or wrong answers; the evaluation should take 10 to 15 minutes.

Basic Imagery Training

Regardless of your scores on the Sport Imagery Questionnaire, you need to practice some basic imagery exercises before you attempt to incorporate imagery into your daily training regimen. As a skill, imagery requires practice to perfect the technique. Even if you scored all "5s," that does not mean you should skip these exercises. Great tennis players continually practice the fundamentals regardless of how talented they are. Of course some of you will require more practice than others; take a cue from your evaluation to determine in which specific areas you need more practice. The specific areas that are included in basic imagery training are vividness and controllability.

Vividness

One of the most important aspects of imagery is the ability to recreate or create as closely as possible the actual experience in your mind. The closer your images are to the real thing, the better the transfer to actual performance. As discussed earlier, good imagers will make use of all their senses and try to make their images as vivid and detailed as possible. That is why it is important to hear, see, and feel the movement as accurately as possible. In addition, experiencing the emotions and thoughts of the actual competition will further improve imagery effectiveness. For example, feeling the anxiety, concentration, anger, or exhilaration associated with your performance helps make the performance more real. The more you can image yourself on the tennis court in a particular match or practice session, the more benefits you will derive. Remember, the body can't tell the difference between real and vividly imagined experiences. The following exercises are designed to improve the vividness, clarity, and detail of your images.

Exercise 1.   Close your eyes. Allow yourself to relax. As you relax, imagine a blank, white screen. On that screen visualize a blue circle: a rich and deep blue circle. Now, let the blue circle gradually fade into a green one. Then, allow the green circle to change to yellow: a smooth, shiny, solid, bright yellow circle. Let the brightness fade out of the yellow and see the color change to a dull amber and on through orange to a deep, dark, rich red. Scatter a bunch of small drops of blue in the red circle and watch them bleed into the red, mixing more and more evenly until the circle is a uniform purple. Now, let the purple get darker and darker until it becomes black: a dark, shiny, bottomless black hole. Take the edges of the black circle and square them off so that your black circle becomes a black square. Let the black circle become gray, gradually getting lighter and lighter until your gray becomes white, leaving you with the same white screen with which you began.

Exercise 2. Once again get comfortable, relax, and close your eyes. Then imagine a pitcher of fruit punch sitting on the kitchen counter. The pitcher is about three-quarters full. It has been sitting on the counter for quite some time, so it is room temperature. Stick your index finger into the liquid. Notice the movement as your finger breaks the surface tension, causing waves of ripples to spread out, bouncing off the inside walls of the glass pitcher. Notice the feel of the punch: wet, tepid, and perhaps slightly sticky with some sugar. Now, bring your finger toward your mouth. The fragrance of the punch on your finger precedes the taste as the remnants of liquid settle on your tongue. Reach into a bucket of ice and fill your fist with ice cubes. Your fingers chill at the touch of the cold, moist ice. Hold your hand over the pitcher and release the ice into the punch. In slow motion, the cubes fall into the liquid, splashing it up. Picking up a long stirring spoon, stir the ice into the punch to cool it off. As you do, listen to the clang of the spoon against the pitcher and watch the whirlpool of colored liquid you have created. Removing the spoon, lift the pitcher and pour yourself a glass of punch. Be sure to notice the flow of the liquid in great detail as it fills the glass. Next, lift the glass and drink the contents. Really experience how it feels to taste the punch. As you swallow, follow the cool liquid as it descends through your esophagus and into your stomach.

Exercise 3. Imagine that you are at home in your living room. Look around and take in all the details: What do you see? Notice the shape and the texture of the furniture. What sounds do you hear? Really be there, looking out. What is the temperature like? Is there any movement in the air? What odors do you smell? Use all your senses to take it all in.

Exercise 4. Select a particular shot and visualize yourself performing it perfectly. I have used the serve as an example, but you can substitute any shot you like once you understand the imagery process.

See and feel yourself performing the serve perfectly. To accomplish this, image yourself in the ready position, looking at your opponent and the service court, and pick the spot where you want the serve to go. See and feel yourself start your service motion and release the ball at the perfect height with the toss going just where you wanted. Feel your back arching and your shoulder stretching as you take the racquet back behind your head. Feel your weight start to transfer forward and your arm and racquet reaching high to contact the ball at just the right height and angle. Feel your wrist snapping as you explode into the ball. Now, see and feel the follow through with your weight coming completely forward. You see the ball going exactly where you wanted it to, forcing a high floating return from your opponent. You close in on the net and put the ball away with a sharp firm crosscourt volley.

Exercise 5.   You are to recall as vividly as possible a time when you performed very well. If you can recall a finest hour in recent memory, use that. Your visualization will cover three specific areas of recall: visual, auditory, and kinesthetic.

In visual recall you are to picture how you look when you're playing well. You should notice that you look different when you are playing well as opposed to when you are playing poorly. You walk differently, carrying your head and shoulders differently. When an athlete is confident on the inside, it shows on the outside. Try to get as clear a picture as possible of what you look like when you are playing well. Reviewing film of past good performances can substantially help to crystallize this visualization.

For auditory recall, listen in your mind to the sounds you hear when you are playing well, particularly the internal dialogue you have with yourself. There is often an internal silence that accompanies your best performances. Listen to it. What is your internal dialogue like? What are you saying to yourself and how are you saying it? What is your internal response when faced with adversity during play? Recreate all the sounds as vividly as possible.

For kinesthetic recall, recreate clearly in your mind all the bodily sensations you have when playing well. How do your feet and hands feel? Do you have a feeling of quickness, looseness, speed, or intensity in your body? Often, your racquet has a distinctive feel when playing well. How does the racquet feel on your forehand, backhand, serve, and volley? Focus on the bodily sensations that are associated with playing well.

Controllability

Another extremely important aspect of successful imagery involves controllability; that is, you must learn to control your images so that they do what you want them to do. Many athletes have reported that they have difficulty controlling their images, often repeating the same mistake again and again. In working with tennis players I have often found that players struggle with controllability. For example, several players have reported that in visualizing their serve, the ball constantly hits just outside the service box; or, they visualize their groundstrokes going into the top of the net. Other players have reported trouble ending a point, constantly imaging their opponents returning the ball, no matter where they hit it. Controlling your image allows you to picture exactly what you want to accomplish instead of seeing yourself making errors. You want to program the body to hit great shots, not to make unforced errors and double faults. The following exercises are designed to help you control your images.

Exercise 1. Imagine yourself holding a tennis ball. Examine it very closely: the color, seams, texture, and any other detail you can imagine. Could you draw in your mind's eye a tennis ball with realistic detail? Now see yourself bouncing the tennis ball and catching it after each bounce. Imagine that you are getting ready to serve and see yourself bouncing the ball as many times as you usually do before serving. See yourself tossing the ball to the exact spot where you want to contact the ball.

Exercise 2. Imagine yourself working on your groundstrokes in practice. First, see and feel yourself hitting all shots crosscourt and deep near the baseline. Pick out a spot on the court and try to hit that spot with your shots. Try this with both slice and topspin shots. Notice the difference in net clearance and the bounce of the ball when hitting topspin and slice. Now see yourself going down the line, again trying to hit it deep and to a particular spot on the court. You can continue to do this for the rest of the shots in your repertoire (i.e., serve, volley, overhead, approach shot, etc.).

Exercise 3. Imagine yourself working on a specific shot that has given you trouble in the past. Take careful notice of what you were doing wrong. Now imagine yourself performing that shot perfectly. See and feel your movements and watch the ball go exactly where you want it to go. For example, see and feel yourself hitting a slice serve wide to the deuce court, beyond the reach of your opponent.

Now, do the same thing, this time thinking about a match situation in which you have had trouble in the past. It might be serving for the match, getting behind early, hitting on second serve under pressure, or making a critical passing shot or overhead shot. Put yourself in this situation and then see yourself staying calm and hitting the successful shots.

Exercise 4. Picture yourself playing against an opponent who has given you trouble in the past. Try to play out points against this person just as you would like them to happen. Imagine a variety of situations and type of points including serve, return of serve, groundstrokes, volley, overhead, and lob. Set up a strategy in your mind about how best to play this person and carry this strategy out in your imagery. For example, you might see yourself exchanging groundstrokes, keeping the ball deep; take the opportunity to approach on a short ball and put away a crisp volley. Make sure you control the choice of shots, the placement of shots, and your positioning and movement. Try to feel what it is like to hit these shots just the way you want to.

Exercise 5. Most tennis players have problems with tensing up, becoming angry, losing concentration, or losing confidence. Picture yourself in a situation that usually brings out one of these emotions. It might be missing an easy overhead, double faulting, losing serve, or making a series of unforced errors. Recreate the situation and especially the feelings that accompany that situation. For example, feel the anxiety of playing in an important match, but use one of the anxiety management strategies discussed previously in chapter 4. Feel the tension drain out of your body and focus on what you need to do to win the next point. Again the focus should be on controlling what you see, hear, and feel in your imagery.

Summary

The psychological skill of imagery is one of the most powerful techniques you have at your disposal to help improve performance. But imagery is much more than just visualizing yourself hitting a forehand or backhand; it should involve also feeling the movement and hearing the sounds of the racquet strike the ball. Imagery is not magic; rather, it works through facilitation of the neural pathways. Remember, the mind does not know the difference between real and imagined events. Imagery can be used to control emotional responses, improve concentration, practice strategy, and build confidence in addition to improving your strokes. Imagery can be done from either an internal or an external perspective depending on your orientation, although internal imagery usually produces a better kinesthetic feel of the movement. Finally, imagery training in vividness and controllability is important in increasing the effectiveness of your imagery. The next chapter presents an imagery training program.

CHAPTER 9

Implementing An Imagery Program

In the previous chapter I discussed the fundamentals of imagery and provided specific exercises to improve the vividness and controllability of your images. Once you become reasonably proficient at experiencing vivid images and controlling them as well as using all your senses and emotions while imaging, you are ready to start a systematic training program. Remember that for imagery to be most effective, it needs to be built into your routine like any other part of practice.

Imagery Training: An Individualized Program

What follows is a list of tips, guidelines, and suggestions for implementing an imagery training program. It is important to remember that imagery programs need to be individualized based on the needs, abilities, and interest of each tennis player. The program need not be complex or cumbersome but should fit nicely into your daily routine. Pick out the things that make the most sense to you and your present situation and start out slowly. As you become more comfortable, add other things to your program.

Find the Right Setting

As a general rule, your imagery should be practiced in a quiet, comfortable setting with a minimum of distractions. Some people like to practice imagery in their rooms before going to sleep, others use imagery in the locker room before playing a match, and still others like to take time out during a break at school or work to practice their imagery. As your imagery skill develops, you will learn to use it in the face of distractions and eventually even during an actual match.

Achieve Relaxed Concentration

In chapter 4 you were taught several different techniques for relaxation. Research has found that imagery preceded by relaxation is more effective than imagery alone. So make sure that prior to every imagery session you try to get relaxed by using progressive relaxation, deep breathing, or any other relaxation procedure. By relaxing your mind and body you can more easily forget your daily worries and concerns and focus your concentration on the task at hand. In addition, a relaxed state will result in more powerful imagery because it won't have to compete with other events.

Have Realistic Expectations and Motivation

One of the problems I have encountered in using imagery with tennis players is the belief that imagery will make them much better players overnight. It is as if they felt that imagery would magically transform them into the player of their dreams. Imagery can improve your skills if you work at it systematically, but don't expect overnight success. Furthermore, imagery can help you reach your potential, but it can't make you a Martina Navratilova or an Ivan Lendl if you have only average skills.

On the other hand, another problem I often face is that some players just don't believe that imagery will help their games. They are skeptical and thus practice it in a haphazard fashion. It is extremely important that you believe that imagery can help because images are generally more vivid when you believe in them. In addition, if imagery is to be effective you must develop your imagery skills in a regular and systematic fashion. This requires dedication and a belief that your imagery training will pay off in improved performance. It requires the same type of motivation as working on changing your backhand or service motion; they all take a great deal of practice, time, and energy with the expectation that your effort will be rewarded in the future.

Use Vivid and Controllable Images

The importance of vividness and controllability cannot be overemphasized as evidenced by the series of training exercises presented earlier. Whenever imaging, you should strive to include as many senses as possible and to feel the movement as if you were there. Creating a real experience will improve the effectiveness of your imagery. In addition, work on trying to control your images so they follow your instructions and produce the desired outcome. Your imagery exercises in these two areas should provide you with the training necessary to accomplish these goals.

For additional help in imagery training, pay particular attention to environmental detail such as the color of the courts, layout of facilities, and positioning of fences and grandstands; these will help you bring greater clarity and detail to your imagery. For example, when playing at a new court it is useful to scope out the courts in advance so that you can practice being there in your imagery. Several Olympic teams visit the actual competition sites months in advance so they can visualize themselves performing in that exact setting. In addition, to help get the actual feel of the stroke in your imagery, try to increase your awareness of what your body feels like when hitting certain shots. You might even practice in front of a mirror to get an awareness of how you look and feel. Your goal again is to make the imagery as real as if you were actually there.

Focus On the Positive—Occasional Failure

When you practice your imagery, generally focus on successful performance. For instance, if you image hitting crosscourt backhands, you should see all your backhands being hit out in front of you and all the shots going deep and crosscourt. Or, if you are playing an actual match in your mind you should see yourself hitting the shots you want to hit and winning the points.

Although you want to focus on positive outcomes and perfect shots occasionally you should see yourself making an error or experiencing a negative outcome. The reason for this is that nobody is a perfect tennis player (although some people believe they should be); we all make mistakes and errors every time we step onto the court. When you make a mistake, it is important to be able to leave the missed shot behind and go on to the next point with a clear mind (as discussed in chapter 5). This can be accomplished through your imagery training by preparing you for the eventuality of making a mistake and effectively coping with the error.

Take, for example, a situation in which you are serving at 4-5, 30-40 and you need a big first serve. You miss your first serve and are left with a potentially very difficult second serve. This is an instructive situation for your imagery training because you can image missing that first serve and, instead of getting nervous and uptight, see yourself taking a deep breath and going through your preservice routine (described in chapter 6). You hit a confident well-placed second serve and go on to win the point and hold your serve. Or, you might occasionally see yourself losing a tough first set. Instead of getting discouraged and mad, you can visualize yourself increasing in determination and concentration. In this image, you can come back to win the match with some inspired play.

The point is that you generally want to imagine successful outcomes because this helps program the body to execute these skills. The more you can visualize successful shots, the stronger your motor program will be. But because errors and mistakes are part of the game you should be prepared to deal effectively with these situations. There may be one or two particular errors or situations from which you have trouble recovering; imagery is a perfect tool to practice coping effectively with these problem areas.

Use Triggers

One of the ways to help tennis players focus on the correct cues during imagery is through the use of triggers. The actual triggers can vary from player to player based on their own particular needs and abilities. The following are examples of how to use triggers in your game.

If you have a ''herky-jerky'' style to your service motion you might use the word *smooth* to emphasize a nice, easy, controlled swing. Or, if you are having trouble getting caught flat-footed on return of serve you might use the cue *forward* to emphasize getting the feet moving and racquet back early. If your footwork is sometimes slow, you might use the word *quick* to emphasize movement. These cues are intended not to be part of your imagery but to serve the purpose of creating and initiating certain types of images.

Use Memory Aids

An effective way to help facilitate your ability to recreate and create images is through the use of memory aids. These are somewhat similar to triggers except that they usually consist of physical objects or other movement experiences that help stimulate your imagery. For example, Bruce Jenner, the 1976 Olympic decathlon champion, kept a hurdle in his living room so that every time he saw it, he would imagine running the hurdles in competition (his weakest event).

Videotapes. In terms of tennis there are a number of memory aids that you might use to help facilitate your imagery. One good aid is the use of videotapes. When I ask tennis players to image their serve, for example, I often get the comment that they can image their teammate's serve because they see it every day but they have trouble with their own serve because they don't know what they look like. This is not surprising, given that it is difficult to visualize something you have never seen. Have someone make a videotape of your playing, including all of your strokes and movements from side to side as well as up and back. If you can, splice the film, picking out only your best shots. This will give you a better picture of how you look when you are hitting the ball. For most players, seeing themselves on videotape for the first time is quite eye-opening as the typical comment is "Is that me?" In fact, videotape can be very helpful in correcting errors because the player can actually see what the problem is rather than simply being told by the coach or pro. Seeing yourself perform gives you a different perspective that is in some ways more meaningful than verbal instructions.

A new program called Sybervision uses this principle. The producers of Sybervision chose a professional tennis player (Stan Smith) to model all the basic strokes, hitting each one perfectly. Along with footage of Smith's perfect shots, the tape also brings in auditory cues, such as the sound of the racquet striking the tennis ball. The one problem I found with Sybervision is that, no matter how perfect Stan Smith's shots are, they are unique to him. Because we all have our own special way of hitting the ball we might benefit more from watching our own great shots rather than Stan Smith's. On the other hand, Sybervision might be right for you if you do not have certain shots in your repertoire or are struggling with a shot. In any case, videotape is a powerful memory aid to help in creating your images.

Cassette tapes. With the increased emphasis on mental preparation, there has been an increasing number of commercially produced imagery tapes to help athletes prepare for competition. Although some of these tapes are of high quality, I believe that a more effective way to use tapes is to make one for yourself (or have your coach or sport psychologist make it). You can make a tape (or tapes) that is specific to your skills, abilities, and special needs. You should probably start out with a couple of minutes of relaxation instructions before starting the imagery. The imagery itself should be as detailed as possible, following the guidelines I have set forth in this chapter. The more specific the image, the better, although you might also make a more general tape that emphasizes the feel of your different strokes which you can use in a variety of situations. Use the verbal cues and triggers to help you produce vivid, controllable images that simulate the actual competitive setting.

Physical cues.   Another way to stimulate your imagery is to go through some actual strokes in slow motion. Pay attention to how it feels at different points in the stroke such as ready position, pivot, backswing, weight shift, forward swing, contact, and follow-through for a typical ground-stroke. Can you feel the tension in your wrist, forearm, and shoulders as you move from one part of the stroke to the next? Can you feel how your feet move throughout the stroke? Can you feel shifts in body weight? All of these will help trigger your imagery at the appropriate times and increase its vividness and detail.

Visual cues.   You can also use visual cues to help develop your imagery. Go out to the court you usually play on in practice or in matches. Take different positions on the court such as serving and returning serve from both the ad and deuce courts, playing from the baseline, playing at net, and approaching the net. At each position, take some time to try to recreate the visual cues that you would ordinarily see during an actual match. The clearer and more detailed your imagery the more powerful the effects on your performance.

Image Both Execution and Outcome

When performing imagery, be sure to image both the execution of your shot and the end result. Many tennis players image the execution of the shot but not where it lands, whereas others see where the shot lands but don't see themselves hitting the ball. To perform this correctly you must be able to feel the movement of the shot and control the image so that the ball lands in the desired location. For instance, if you were working on your crosscourt slice backhand you would try to feel what it is like to hit that particular shot, paying close attention to footwork, position, racquet angle, weight transfer, and follow-through. Then you would see the ball clear the net and bounce deep near the baseline across the court.

Image in Real Time

Another important point to remember when performing imagery is to try to image in real time. In other words, the time spent imaging a particular shot or situation should be the same amount as the time it actually takes to accomplish this act on the court. If you are working on your serve (including your preservice routine), for example, and in actuality this takes 10 seconds, then your image of the serve should be exactly 10 seconds long.

To see how long certain shots or points take, have someone come out to the court with a stopwatch and record how long you normally take to serve, return serve, hit your groundstrokes, and play points; the time should include how long you usually take between points. Most tennis players tend to image faster than the actual time it takes to perform the skill. It is important to image in real time because you want the transfer from your imagery to real life to be as easy as possible. If your imagery is not performed according to real time, the benefits to your timing and coordination will be less likely to transfer over to your actual tennis playing.

To practice your awareness of real time in your images, time yourself as you do simple things around the house like walking from room to room, or walking out to the mailbox and back, or taking the dog for a walk. After you time yourself, image those activities to see if your imagery takes the same amount of time.

Use Internal Imagery If Possible

As discussed previously, there are two basic types of imagery: internal and external. Although both types have been shown to be effective in improving performance, several studies (Hale[1]; Harris & Robinson[2]) indicate that an internal perspective tends to produce the greatest effects. This is primarily because internal imagery involves performing from your own perspective, and thus it is much easier to be aware of how the body feels while hitting the tennis ball. Furthermore, the electrical activity in the muscles performing the skill is greater when imaging from an internal perspective. Because imagery works by facilitating muscular activity and helping the skill become more automatic, it makes sense that internal imagery would make it easier to accomplish this goal.

Don't worry if you have trouble with internal imagery. Some people either tend naturally to image externally or are not comfortable with internal imagery. If this is a problem for you, it is quite appropriate to use an external perspective. Providing it is clear, detailed, and controllable, your image will be effective. It is also possible to switch back and forth from internal to external imagery depending on the nature of the skill and the particular situation.

Use Imagery to Strengthen as Well as Correct

Many tennis players make the mistake of using imagery only to correct errors or flaws in their game. Usually, players first turn to imagery when they are having a problem with a particular stroke or are having trouble at specific points in a match like falling behind early, failing to close out a match, becoming nervous or tentative, or losing concentration. Although imagery most certainly can be helpful in these cases, it should not be limited to correcting problems. Imagery can help also strengthen your muscle memory of those shots and situations that you already perform well. If you already have a great serve, this does not mean that you can forget about it and not practice it regularly. The same principle holds true for your imagery. A good time to practice this is right after coming off the court when you have played well (or at least done some things very well). You should still have a clear picture of how the good shots felt; this will make it easier to image as well as making the imagery more powerful.

Practice Strategies as Well as Strokes

As discussed briefly earlier in the chapter, it is useful to practice strategies for upcoming matches as well as practicing your various strokes. Many

tennis players I have worked with like to observe their opponent in a prior match, making mental notes concerning their tendencies (e.g., Do they like to go crosscourt or down the line on passing shots? Do they serve and volley or stay back? Do they have any obvious weaknesses?) and the ways they respond to certain situations. With this information in mind, you could imagine playing your opponent, mentally trying to hit different shots from different positions on the court. Try to see yourself successfully carrying out your specific strategy as you take advantage of your strengths and your opponent's weaknesses. In addition, you could also visualize counterattacking your opponent's best weapons such as a good, low return of serve against a big serve and volley player.

When to Use Imagery

One of the most often asked questions concerns when to use imagery. Although imagery can be used at virtually any time, there are some specific times when it is most useful.

Before and After Practice

As has been suggested, imagery should be used systematically and regularly to gain the maximum benefits. One way to help accomplish this is to use imagery before and after each practice session. These sessions should be generally about 10 minutes in length because many players have trouble concentrating on their imagery for longer periods of time.

Before practice, visualize the different strokes, drills, and exercises you will be performing. Keep in mind the principles about seeing, feeling, and hearing in your imagery. This serves to get your mind on tennis and to warm up the nervous system to play at top efficiency.

It is also appropriate to practice imagery after each practice session for 10 minutes. At this time, review the shots and strategies you worked on in practice. Because you just finished working out, the feel of your strokes and movement should be fresh in your mind; this will help you to create even clearer and more detailed imagery.

Before and After Matches

Imagery is a good way to get your mind focused on an upcoming match. This allows you to go over in your mind exactly how you want to play the match, setting up your strategy for different situations. As in imagery before practice, imagery before a match helps get the nervous system working to fine-tune your strokes.

The appropriate time to use imagery before the match depends on individual preferences. Some players like to visualize right before going out on the court whereas others like to start an hour or two before the match. The important point is that the imagery should fit comfortably into your prematch routine (discussed in detail in chapter 12). You might even use your imagery at two or three different times, such as two hours, one hour, and 30 minutes, before the match for 10 minutes at a time. If you use several sessions, you can work on your strategy in one of them and then try to get the feel of your strokes in another. The prematch possibilities for imagery are many and, ultimately, depend on personal preference.

An often overlooked time for using imagery is right after a match. With the match clearly in your mind, you can replay the shot and points that you performed successfully, really getting a vivid, controllable image. In addition, you can replay the unsuccessful points or strokes in the match, imagining yourself performing successfully or choosing a different shot or strategy. For example, if you lost several critical points staying at the baseline, replay those points and picture yourself being patient but coming to net on short balls and putting away a volley or overhead.

Before Serve and Service Return

Due to the nature of the game, there is not really enough time to image during a match except before serving and returning serve when there is a break in the action. Imaging can be a part of your service and service return routines as discussed in chapter 6. Of course, before you can use imagery during a match, you'll have to practice it so that it becomes a natural part of your routine before serving and returning serve.

During Changeovers

The longest free time during the course of a match occurs during changeovers. This is the time when most players try to catch their breath and conserve some energy, particularly during a tough match on a hot day. This time can also be used effectively by incorporating imagery into your routine. After catching your breath and getting a drink, sit in a chair (or on the ground) and visualize what you would like to do in the upcoming two games. If you will be serving, see yourself succeeding in your first serve and following it to net; if you will be returning serve, picture yourself hitting your returns in front of you, keeping the ball low at your opponent's feet as that person rushes the net. Finally, you might use your imagery to decide how you want to play the next game including your choice and placement of shots. In any case, imagery is a useful tool to use during changeovers, a time that is not used effectively by many players.

At Home

Besides using imagery in the various situations I have described above, it can also be used at home (or any other appropriate quiet place). It may be difficult to find a quiet spot before practicing, and there may be many days when you do not practice at all. Consequently, practice your imagery at home when you have some quiet time. It is useful to try to set aside 10 to 15 minutes at a particular time in the day so that this becomes your routine. Some players like to do it just before they go to sleep, whereas others prefer to practice imagery after dinner. Again, the important point is to have a set time every day for imagery so that you can practice it regularly without interruption.

Use Imagery Logs

One good way to keep track of how much and how often you are using imagery is to keep an imagery log for each day. The log should contain information concerning how long you imaged, what you imaged, when you imaged, and how vivid and controlled your images were. This will provide you with important feedback as well as highlighting the importance of consistent, systematic practice.

Summary

Chapter 9 has presented guidelines for the implementation of an imagery training program. To review, a basic individual imagery program includes the following recommended ingredients.

1. Evaluate your imagery ability (chapter 8)
2. Practice making the images vivid, controllable, emotional, and kinesthetic using the exercises provided (chapters 8 and 9)
3. Use imagery (chapter 9)
   a. before practice
   b. after practice
   c. before matches
   d. after matches
   e. as part of serve and return of serve routines
   f. during changeovers
   g. regularly at home
4. Keep a daily imagery log.

Of course, the best imagery program is one that is tailored to the particular needs of each player. You need to design the program that best suits your needs and schedule. Remember that a strong belief in your imagery program is extremely important for its ultimate success. Improvement will not come overnight, but if you stay on a regular schedule and include imagery as part of your daily training regimen, you will be setting yourself up for increased success in the future.

CHAPTER 10

Psychological Skill #5: Building Confidence

The whole thing is never to get negative about yourself. Sure, it's possible that the other guy you're playing is tough, and that he may have beaten you the last time you played, and okay, maybe you haven't been playing all that well yourself. But the minute you start thinking about these things you're dead. I go out to every match convinced that I'm going to win. That is all there is to it.[1]

Jimmy Connors
(before playing Bjorn Borg in the finals of the U. S. Open).

A very strange thing happened. Even though I didn't give myself much of a chance against Connors, when the newspaper reporters and everyone asked me what was going to happen (if it came down to Connors and me in the final), I had to tell them that, of course, I thought I was going to win. So they started asking me why, and I started to think up reasons. And the more I thought about the reasons—especially the fact that I had Davis Cup experience and Jimmy didn't—the more I began to realize that I really was going to win. And when I finally went out to the court, I was very confident.[2]

Raul Ramirez
(before playing Jimmy Connors in the North American Zone Davis Cup finals—Ramirez went on to upset Connors).

The above comments capture the critical role that confidence plays in a tennis player's mental outlook and ultimate success. The importance of confidence is further evidenced by tennis players' comments indicating that it is one of the psychological states present when they are playing at the top of their game (see chapter 2). In fact, research has indicated that the most consistent factor distinguishing highly successful from less successful tennis players is confidence: Top players display a strong belief in their abilities.

The purpose of this chapter is to explore the elusive yet critical concept of confidence. First, I present a definition of confidence along with its characteristics. Second, I discuss some important points concerning how confidence can affect performance, effort, and persistence. Third, I explore the notions of overconfidence and underconfidence. Fourth, I discuss how to increase awareness of your feelings of confidence. And finally, I present several suggestions for building your confidence.

Self-Confidence—What Is It?

Tennis players describing their wins and losses say things like: ''I just didn't feel confident in my backhand,'' ''I really felt confident in my serve,'' ''I felt confident that I could come back from behind,'' and ''I just never felt confident that I could break serve.'' Although the term confidence is used frequently, few people can define exactly what confidence is. This is how Roy Emerson describes confidence.

> *The whole thing is to have a positive mental approach. You can see it in a player like John Newcombe. When Newcombe is serving well, you can feel the confidence across the other side of the net. He's not worried about the ball going in; he's just blasting away. The worst thing you can do on a court is to say to yourself: ''Do I hit this serve with everything I have, or do I have to get it in?'' You can't think in these terms. You have to make up your mind that you're going to hit the bloody serve and go ahead and hit it.* [3]

Although this is one player's description of confidence it is not a definition of the term. Although there are various definitions of confidence, the consensus from sport psychologists is that *confidence is simply the belief that you can successfully perform a desired behavior*. That behavior might be serving an ace, hitting a passing shot, or defeating an opponent. Confidence is believing in yourself and your abilities. The most significant self-confidence, however, is believing in your ability to acquire the necessary skills and competencies, both physical and mental, to reach your potential as a tennis player. Confident players expect to be successful and

believe in their capacity to perform the actions necessary to be successful. Conversely, players who lack confidence don't expect to win and doubt
their abilities at important points in the match. This type of thinking psychologically limits these players because expectations can have a profound
impact on performance.

Putting Psychological Limits on Ourselves

Your self-confidence has been defined as your expectation of success or
failure. When you doubt your ability to succeed, win a match, or acquire
a new skill, you are creating what is called a self-fulfilling prophecy. This
means that expecting something to happen causes it to happen. Unfortunately, many tennis players never reach their potential because they doubt
their ability. Self-fulfilling prophecies lead to a vicious cycle, in which
players expect to fail; this expectation causes them to fail, confirming their
negative self-image and, in turn, increasing their expectations of failure.
In general, the end result is that we place psychological limits on our performance and thus never believe that we can beat certain players or learn
new strokes.

A classic example of placing psychological limits on athletic performance
occurred in track and field when nobody could break the four-minute mile.
Runners would run 4:03, 4:02, and 4:01, but nobody could crack the four-
minute barrier. In fact, a book was published which stated that it was phys-
iologically impossible to break the four-minute mile. Although most runners believed this, Roger Bannister, a very talented and courageous runner,
did not. He was sure that he could break the four-minute barrier under
the right conditions, and so he did. Although this was an impressive athletic feat, in the next year more than a dozen runners broke the four-minute
mile. Why should this occur? Did everyone all of a sudden train harder
or get faster? The answer is no. What did happen is that runners believed
it could be done! Until Roger Bannister succeeded, runners had been placing
psychological limits on themselves because they felt that it just wasn't possible to break the four-minute mile.

The powerful effects of our expectations or beliefs can also be seen in
our daily lives. Research has shown that giving people a sugar pill for
extreme pain (telling them that it was morphine) produced just as much
relief as actually giving them a pain killer like morphine. Studies have
indicated also the importance of expectations on academic achievement
with students expecting to do well performing better than students not expecting to do well although there was no difference in I.Q. In fact, it was

shown that if teachers expected certain students to improve their academic achievement, these students did indeed show the most improvement.[4]

These ideas have potential application to tennis in that the belief in abilities is critical to success. It's easy to get down on yourself after you have lost several matches in a row or have failed to beat a particular opponent. The importance of keeping your confidence and believing in yourself is highlighted by Rod Laver's remarks:

> *You get into winning or losing patterns. A lot of it's getting the breaks. If you win a lot of close matches, your attitude when you get into close matches is, "No sweat, I've been here before and I'll be here again." But if you start to lose a lot of close ones, or you get ahead in a match, then the whole picture changes. The other guy starts to catch up and you start to think, "Oh, oh, here it comes again." Basically, I think this is what happened to Stan Smith. He lost just enough of the edge so that the close ones he used to win he began losing, and that changed his entire attitude about his game.[5]*

Characteristics of Confidence

Being confident and displaying a confident attitude can help your game in a variety of ways.

Confidence Arouses Positive Emotions

Confidence frees you up for strong, quick, and fluid execution of strokes. In fact, when you are confident, you are more likely to remain calm and relaxed under pressure resulting in not being tentative and going for your shots.

Confidence Facilitates Concentration

Confidence helps to focus your attention on the match. Since you are not trying to avoid failure (which comes with lack of confidence), you are free to concentrate on the task at hand. When you lack confidence, you tend to worry about how well you are doing or how the match will turn out rather than concentrating on each point.

Confidence Affects Your Goals

With confidence, you set challenging goals for yourself and actively pursue those goals. Confidence allows you to reach for the stars and realize your potential. Players who are not confident will tend to set easy goals and therefore never really push themselves to their limits. A thorough discussion of goal setting will be provided in chapter 11.

Confidence Increases Persistence and Effort

One of the most consistent findings is that confidence is one of the major determinants of the extent of a player's effort and persistence. My colleagues and I (Weinberg, Gould, & Jackson[6]) have conducted several research studies in which people of equal ability were distinguished by either having or lacking confidence. Results consistently showed that, in a muscular endurance task, the confident individuals tried harder and persisted longer than the people lacking confidence. With ability equalized, the winners of competitions are usually those players who believe in themselves.

Confidence Affects Shot Selection

One of the major factors that determines the outcome of many tennis matches is shot selection on critical points. Although many players have all the strokes, it's the ability to hit a passing shot, aggressive volley, or big serve at key points in a match that separates the great from the good players. It is not unusual to find players pushing the ball on important shots and hoping their opponent will make an error. But this type of play is only successful up to a point. Usually, confident players will not only choose the right shot but also hit it with authority. Rather than swinging wildly from the heels, the confident player takes normal swings, follows through, and stays relaxed.

Jimmy Connors is probably the best example of a confident player who goes for his shots. But this style of play did not come about by accident. When Connors was growing up, his mother, Gloria, and his grandmother taught him to hit out on the big points, and to never hold back, because that was the only way to become a champion. Connors has mentioned many times that his confidence stemmed from the great support he received from his mother, who never let him lose confidence in himself. This has been evidenced time and time again as we have all seen Jimmy Connors go for the lines and hit out no matter how important the match or how close the score.

Confidence Affects Psychological Momentum

One of the most important effects that confidence has on tennis players is how well they react to adversity. As we all know, momentum in a tennis match can change virtually on one shot. Take the example of the

Ivan Lendl-Jimmy Connors final match at the U. S. Open in 1983. The sets were even at 1-1 and Lendl was serving in the 3rd set and had set point on Connors. Lendl proceeded to double-fault and quickly lost that set and seemingly gave up in the 4th set losing 6-0. Two years later Lendl was again in the finals of the U. S. Open, this time against John McEnroe. McEnroe was holding serve comfortably and was serving for the 1st set when Lendl broke him with a couple of great returns and passing shots. These great shots gave Lendl confidence that he could in fact win, and that McEnroe wasn't unbeatable. Lendl proceeded to win the match in straight sets in an awesome display of power tennis.

If you look at your own tennis matches, I'm sure you would agree that momentum can change very quickly. The ability to change or shift momentum depends a great deal on your self-confidence. Confident players' expectancy of success remains high even if they find themselves behind. They do not give up until the last point is lost. A good case in point was the U. S. Open match between Guillermo Vilas and Manuel Orantes. Vilas won the first two sets and was up 5-1 in the third, but Orantes miraculously came back to win the match—an incredible comeback. In fact, Orantes went on to defeat Jimmy Connors in the finals.

I became interested in how tennis players react to adversity. Thus, my colleagues and I conducted a study in which adversity was defined as losing the first set (in a two-out-of-three set match).[7] Losing the first set is a good test of a player's ability to overcome psychological momentum and come back to win the match. The results of approximately 20,000 USTA matches of male and female players from the under 12's to the professionals produced some interesting results. First, in general, players were not very successful in winning the match after losing the first set, with the loser of the first set winning the match only 12% of the time. Second, when comparing men with women, the results showed that after losing the first set, men came from behind to win the match 14% of the time whereas women came back to win only 8% of the time. Thus men seemed to be able to reverse the momentum more often than women although neither was likely to win the match after losing the first set.

In a follow-up study,[8] we wanted to see if these findings would hold up for the top players in the world. We looked at the top 20 ranked male and female professional players. Interestingly, there was no difference between the men and women with both groups coming from behind to win after losing the first set approximately 37% of the time. This is far greater than the 12% we found in our first study.

So, the question remains: Why can the top players in the world come back to win so much more often than other talented players? The answer appears to lie in the elusive concept of confidence. Of course, the top 20 players have great physical talent, but, then again, so do many other players. Our studies have suggested that one of the most consistent differences that separates the top players from the rest is their belief in their own abilities. This conclusion is based on the fact that when they lose the first set, top players generally do not throw in the towel, convinced that they can't win. On the contrary, they see the situation as a challenge and usually put forth more effort and determination to try to win the match. Confident players never give up until the final point is lost, and the great champions rarely, if ever, lose their confidence. Many players used to say that when Bjorn Borg lost the first two sets (in a three out of five match), that's when he was at his best. For most other players, losing the first two sets would break their spirit and confidence. In general, a high level of confidence and a belief in your ability will help you react favorably to adverse situations.

Confidence Does Not Replace Competence

Many of the previous characteristics of confidence have stressed the critical role that confidence can have concerning your performance. It is important to note, however, that confidence alone will not transform you into a great player. You can be the most confident person in the world but if you have a weak backhand, tentative volleys, an erratic serve, and a slow response, don't expect to be competing at Wimbledon next year. But what confidence can do for you is allow you to come closer to reaching your potential as a player. Take the example of Ivan Lendl, obviously an extremely talented player who had trouble winning big matches in Grand Slam events. With the addition of a lot of negative press, this started to erode his confidence. However, after his victory against John McEnroe in the 1985 U. S. Open he became a totally different player. That victory gave him the confidence he needed to become number one in the world; he was virtually unbeatable in the ensuing months. Although there is no substitute for talent, confidence can be a key to unlock that talent inside you.

Confidence and Performance

I have stressed the point that confidence is a critical factor in determining your performance. I have not really addressed, however, the specific relationship between confidence and performance. This relationship is similar to the relationship between anxiety and performance (see chapter 3).

That is, there is an inverted-U relationship between confidence and performance (See Figure 10.1). Performance improves as your level of confidence increases up to an optimal point, whereupon further increases in confidence will produce a decline in performance.

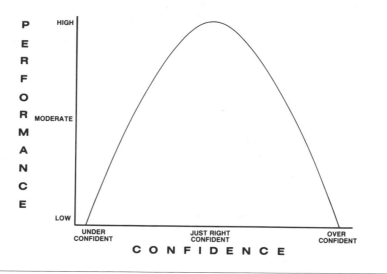

Figure 10.1   Confidence-Performance Relationship

Having optimal self-confidence means that you possess the total conviction that you can achieve your goals and that you will strive hard to do so. As we have stressed, self-confidence does not necessarily mean you will always perform well, but you will not perform well without it; confidence is essential for you to reach your potential. Being confident does not mean that you won't make errors, choke, or lose matches. But having a strong belief in yourself will help you deal with errors effectively and keep you striving toward success.

The view that there is an optimal level of self-confidence of course means that a player can have too little or too much confidence. Let us take a look at the characteristics and effects of under- and overconfidence.

Lack of Confidence

I have previously discussed how we can put psychological limits on ourselves when we lack confidence in our abilities. Unfortunately, this is a problem I encounter a great deal in working with tennis players. Although they have all the strokes, many players lack confidence in their ability to hit these strokes under match conditions, particularly in tight matches. How many times have you seen players warm up, hitting beautiful, deep groundstrokes; crisp, firm volleys; and powerful serves only to start pushing the ball when the match starts?

Many times, lack of confidence is tied to a specific stroke or certain circumstances rather than one's entire game. For instance, some players lose confidence when they fall behind or lose their serve. Other players have trouble closing out a match as they lack confidence in their ability to continue playing well. Yet others lack confidence in a particular stroke (e.g., backhand passing shot or overhead) and this becomes obvious under pressure. Julie Anthony, formerly a professional tennis player and currently a sport psychologist, speaks about having confidence in a particular shot.

My feeling about confidence is that if you've got one big shot you can really count on, it tends to carry over to the rest of your game. One of the reasons I think there are more genuinely confident men players than women players is that a lot of men players have tremendous confidence in their serves. So when the serve is working, they figure the worst they can do is stay even. Most women don't have that luxury. [9]

Overconfidence

The opposite of an underconfident player is the player who is overconfident. As a general rule, this is not as problematic as underconfidence, but when it does occur the effects can be just as devastating. I should note first, however, that the term *overconfidence* is a misnomer: You cannot really be overconfident if your confidence is based on skill and ability. Overconfident players are actually those who are falsely confident, believing that they are better than their actual abilities. The following quote by Bobby Riggs after his match against Billie Jean King reflects this point.

It was mainly a case of overconfidence on my part. I overestimated myself. I underestimated Billie Jean's ability to meet the pressure. I let her pick the surface and the ball because I figured it wouldn't make any difference, that she would beat herself. Even when she won the first set, I wasn't worried. In fact, I tried to bet more money on myself. But I miscalculated. I ran out of gas. She started playing better and better. I started playing worse. I tried to slow up the game to keep her back but she kept the pressure on. [10]

One of the common situations in which overconfidence comes into play is when two players of different abilities play each other. The better player will often approach the match with false confidence, believing that it will be easy to beat the less skillful player. This overconfidence leads to haphazard playing which may well cause the better player (as far as skill level) to fall behind early in the match. The opponent gains confidence in the game, making it even harder for the overconfident player to come back and win the match. Even the best players fall prey to looking past early round opponents and find themselves watching the rest of the tournament from the grandstands. Chris Evert, however, does not underestimate her early round opponents. Over a 15-year period, she has reached at least the semi-finals in 44 of 45 Grand Slam tournaments! This unbelievable consistency can be attributed, in part, to Chris Evert's lack of false confidence. This should serve as an example for all tennis players to follow.

Increasing Awareness of Our Confidence

Having learned that there is an optimal level of confidence and that performance can be hurt by overconfidence and underconfidence, you can now begin to work toward building your self-confidence. The first step is to become more aware of your feelings of confidence including any potential areas of improvement. One way to do this is to pay attention to how you react in a variety of situations. Some of the questions you might ask yourself include:

- When does self-doubt occur?
- How do I recover from mistakes?
- Am I afraid to hit certain shots?
- Do I really expect to play well?
- How do I react to adversity?
- Does my confidence change throughout a match?
- When am I overconfident?
- Do I enjoy tough, tight matches?

The answers to these questions will help you locate your strengths and weaknesses in terms of confidence. Table 10.1 is a questionnaire that will provide you with a more detailed assessment of your self-confidence in tennis.

To score your overall confidence, add up the percentages in each of the three columns and then divide each by 17. The higher your score on the "Confident Just Right" column the more likely you are to be at your optimal level of confidence during a match. High scores on "Not Confident Enough" or "Confident Too Much" present some potential problem areas. To get a feel for your specific strengths and weaknesses, look at each item. Notice that the scale assesses confidence concerning both your physical and your mental skills. Use this information to work on some of the areas where you are not as confident as you would like to be. The following are some suggestions to help you build your confidence.

Table 10.1 Tennis Confidence Inventory

This inventory will help you to evaluate your confidence about various characteristics of yourself that are important to being successful in tennis. As you know athletes can have too little confidence, too much confidence, or just about the right degree of confidence. Read each question carefully and think about your confidence with regard to each item as you competed over the last year. For each item indicate the percent of time you feel you have had too little, too much, or just the right degree of confidence. Below is an example to give you some idea how to fill out the inventory correctly.

	Not Confident Enough	Confidence Just Right	Too Much Confidence
How confident are you that you will get 50% of your first serves in?	20%	70%	10% = 100%

The total percent for all three answers should always be 100%. You may distribute this 100% any way you think is appropriate. You may assign all 100% to one category, split it beween two categories, or, as in the example, divide it among all three categories. Remember you are to indicate the percent of time when you compete that you feel you have too little, just about the right amount, or too much confidence.

With respect to your ability . . .	Not Confident Enough	Confidence Just Right	Too Much Confidence
1. To win from the baseline	____%	____%	____%
2. To make critical decisions in a match	____%	____%	____%
3. To concentrate throughout a match	____%	____%	____%
4. To perform under pressure	____%	____%	____%
5. To serve and volley	____%	____%	____%
6. To return serve successfully	____%	____%	____%
7. To hit winners on your overhead	____%	____%	____%

(Cont.)

Table 10.1   (Cont.)

8. To control your emotions during a match	___ %	___ %	___ %
9. To come from behind and win	___ %	___ %	___ %
10. To improve your game	___ %	___ %	___ %
11. To hit forehand passing shots	___ %	___ %	___ %
12. To hit backhand passing shots	___ %	___ %	___ %
13. To consistently serve well	___ %	___ %	___ %
14. To successfully approach the net	___ %	___ %	___ %
15. To anticipate your opponent's shots	___ %	___ %	___ %
16. To put forth the effort to succeed	___ %	___ %	___ %
17. To execute successful strategy	___ %	___ %	___ %
Total	___ %	___ %	___ %
Total/17	___ %	___ %	___ %

Building Confidence

Many tennis players make the mistake of thinking that there is nothing they can do to build their confidence. In keeping with the theme of the book, however, I will show you how you can build confidence through work, practice, and planning. For example, as discussed earlier, Jimmy Connors' mother carefully planned his career as a junior to make sure he did not lose his confidence. She taught Connors to hit out, and, because of this, he lost some matches while growing up that he probably should have won. But Connors says he could never have made it without his mother and grandmother. *"They were so sensational in their support, they never allowed me to lose confidence. They just kept telling me to play the same way, and they kept assuring me that it would eventually come together. And I believed them."*[11] Although other people are helpful in building your confidence, you should know that you don't have to rely on them to become a confident tennis player; there are things you can do yourself. The remainder of the chapter is devoted to presenting strategies, techniques, and suggestions for improving your confidence.

Performance Accomplishments

Research has indicated that the most powerful builder of confidence is performance accomplishments. Basically, this means having performed a behavior successfully in the past will increase your confidence that you can perform it successfully again in the future. The behavior might take the form of beating a particular opponent, coming from behind to win, hitting a down-the-line backhand passing shot under pressure, or hitting a drop volley. Successfully performing these actions give you confidence to perform them again.

Of course, this is not always as easy as it sounds. If you have lost 10 straight matches to a tough opponent, it will be hard to be confident in the next match. You know that confidence is crucial to success, but how can you be confident without previous success? The relationship between confidence and success becomes a "Catch-22" situation: Do you need to be confident to win or do you need to win to become confident? This dilemma is captured by Brian Gottfried who was in the midst of a hot streak, *"I'm winning now because I'm confident, but the reason I'm confident is that I'm winning."*[12]

In response to this dilemma, research has found that, for the most part, performance accomplishments build confidence, and confidence then improves subsequent performances. Nothing elicits confidence like experiencing in practice what you want to accomplish in a match. You are likely to have little doubt about your capability of hitting a certain shot if you have consistently hit that shot in practice.

Although this seems logical, it is not as easy as it seems. It is quite possible to hit beautiful strokes in practice but fall to pieces in a match. The reasons for this are many, but it is most likely that you really are not confident about that particular stroke. If you were truly confident, you could maintain that confidence, regardless of the importance of a match. So what can you do to increase your confidence through performance accomplishments?

First, it is possible that you need to put more time and practice into perfecting that particular stroke (the serve, for example) so that you feel totally comfortable with it. This may require you to hit 100 serves during each practice, working on first and second serves as well as hitting to the ad and deuce courts. But because serving in a match is different from serving 100 balls, you should try to work on your serve under match conditions, playing each point out. Further, a match involves pressure and this can affect your serve; so, set up specific situations like serving at 4-4, 30-40, or 5-4, 15-40 to simulate game conditions. The more success you have with your serve under a variety of conditions, the more confidence you will have in it during a match.

I have shown you how to work on different strokes and create different situations to build your confidence. Unfortunately, it is not likely that you will be able to play your arch rival in practice. How can you build your confidence if you have lost to a given opponent repeatedly? The answer is with imagery.

Image Success

In chapter 8 I indicated that one of the uses of imagery was to help build confidence. One of the great things about imagery is that you can see yourself beating an opponent whom you have never defeated before. Losing consistently to a particular individual is certainly discouraging. You can defeat the opponent by imaging that you are successful and that you carry out your game plan to perfection. You can also image how to react to situations that have given you trouble in the past. For example, if you have had trouble returning serve, you might see yourself shortening up your backswing and just stepping in and hitting crisp, low returns. Or, if you are getting passed often, visualize yourself hitting good, deep approach shots and then finishing off the points with crisp, deep volleys. In any case, imagery can help provide you with a feeling of success and confidence that might otherwise not be available to you.

Act Confidently

One of the best and easiest ways to build confidence is to act confidently. Since your thoughts, feelings, and behaviors all affect one another, the more you act confidently, the more likely you are to feel and think confidently. This is especially important when you begin to lose confidence, and your opponent, sensing this, begins to gain confidence.

Always try to display a confident image on the court. Unfortunately, many players give themselves away by their body language and movements, which indicate when they are lacking confidence. In fact, a recent study that videotaped hundreds of matches found that in most cases, an observer could tell who was winning and losing just by the way the players walked and moved between points.

Acting confidently not only makes you feel better but also can be very disconcerting to your opponent. Players like Chris Evert and Bjorn Borg never let you know if they were not feeling confident (which probably wasn't very often). Their expressions, movements, and mannerisms remained constant regardless of whether they were winning 5-1 or losing

5-1. This told their opponents that they had everything under control and were not worried about losing. Most players look for some negative reaction from their opponent which signals that they have lost confidence, desire, or hope because this fuels their own confidence. But Chris Evert and Bjorn Borg gave no such signals.

Acting confidently can also keep your spirits up, even during difficult times during a match. If you walk around with slumped shoulders, dragged racquet, head down, and pained facial expression, you communicate to all observers that you are down, and this also works to pull you further down. So, keep your head up, shoulders back, racquet head up, and facial muscles loose and indicate that you are confident and still fighting for the match. This will help your attitude as well as keep your opponent guessing as to how you feel.

Think Confidently

One of the most important aspects of confidence is to think confidently. This goes back to the material presented in chapter 7 on self-talk. Confidence largely consists of thinking that you can and will achieve your goals. If you think confidently, your body is more likely to react in a confident manner. As one tennis player I worked with said, *"If I think I can win, I'm awfully tough to beat."*

Keeping a positive attitude is essential if you want to be a successful tennis player. That means eliminating all the negative things you say to yourself such as *"I'm so stupid," "I can't believe I'm playing so bad," "I'll never get better,"* and *"I can't beat this person,"* and changing these to positive thoughts, such as *"I can hang in there," "One point doesn't make a match," "Just watch the ball,"* and *"I can beat this person."* These positive thoughts should be instructive rather than judgmental (see chapter 7). Although this is sometimes difficult to do, the result will be a more enjoyable and successful tennis experience.

Be in Good Physical Condition

In order to feel confident on the court you must be in the best physical shape possible. Until recently, this has been an overlooked aspect of tennis, particularly in women's tennis. It used to be enough just to play tennis to stay in shape, but people like Martina Navratilova, Chris Evert, Ivan Lendl, and Guillermo Vilas have demonstrated that lifting weights, running, using conditioning exercises, and following good nutrition habits are all part of being in top physical shape. It gives you confidence to know that you can stay on the court all day if necessary to win a match. In interviews, Jack Nicklaus has said, *"As long as I'm prepared, I always expect to win,"* or as one tennis player said, *"You can't be confident without doing the training."*

So make sure your training program builds strength, endurance, speed, flexibility, and quickness as well as stroke efficiency and strategy development. Many players have now realized that they are cheating themselves if they enter a match without the proper preparation. Being prepared gives you confidence that you have done everything possible to ensure success.

Have a Plan of Attack

Many players neglect to build confidence by going onto the court with no plan of attack or strategy. You should always have a plan of attack. Rather than a strategy for how you will hit every shot, a plan of attack requires that you have a general idea of what you want to accomplish and how you want to accomplish it. Having a plan gives you a measure of confidence going into a match because you know what you're going to try to do. Marty Riessen, a former Davis Cup player, speaks to this point.

You always go into a match with a general idea of how the other guy can hurt you, and you try to fix on a couple of things. You think back to the last time you played someone and you try to figure out what went wrong—whether he beat you or you beat yourself. If he was beating you with better shots, it means you've got to figure out a way to pres-

sure him more. So maybe you'll go in with the idea of attacking more than you usually do. If you beat yourself, you may think about just keeping the ball in play. But you have to keep it general because you never know once you get into a match how his strokes are going to be working and how your own strokes are going to work. [13]

Although Riessen's point about a general game plan is well taken, there are certain situations where a more specific play is appropriate. Recall the example of Arthur Ashe's plan against Jimmy Connors in the 1975 Wimbledon final. Because Connors loves pace, Ashe decided to hit "a lot of junk." In addition, he decided to slice his serve wide to Connors' two-handed backhand to open up the court despite the fact that this was one of Connors' strengths. Ashe believed in his strategy and executed it perfectly to pull off a great upset.

Evaluate your strengths and weaknesses along with your opponent's style of play and devise a plan of attack that you believe in. This will help your confidence and give you a clear picture of what to do once you get into the match.

Establishing a Prematch Routine

A consistent prematch routine reduces stress and anxiety while helping you concentrate on the upcoming match. Knowing exactly what will happen and when it will happen gives you confidence and puts your mind at ease. Knowing when you will eat, practice, stretch out, and arrive at the courts helps to build confidence in your prematch preparation. I discuss this in more detail in chapter 12.

Play Good Players—Not Superior Players

A common fallacy is believing that you should always try to play people better than yourself; the reasoning being that a superior player will help you raise the level of your game to compete with them. Although there is nothing wrong with playing superior competition, doing only this can have negative long-term consequences. Specifically, if you are always overmatched, you will be losing constantly. In this situation, you are learning how to lose, and thus your confidence is broken. Try to structure your matches so that you have a realistic chance for success; you need to learn how to win as well as how to lose.

Stay Confident When Opponent Is Playing Well

One of the most discouraging times as a tennis player is when you are playing pretty well but your opponent can't miss. Even though you might be doing all the right things, your opponent seems to have all the answers. Your confidence can really take a beating if you don't handle the situation correctly. Many players just give up because they feel they can't possibly win. Or, sometimes they try to go for low percentage shots not in their repertoire, believing that this is the only way they can win a point. Both these tactics ultimately will lead to failure.

A confident tennis player realizes that players go through hot streaks, but usually will cool off after a few games or a set. It is rare that a player can sustain incredible shot making throughout a match. The key is to keep the level of your game high so that when your opponent falters, you are right there to take advantage of the situation. This can be difficult because you might be losing points and games due to your opponent's great shots. Confident players know that if they keep the pressure on, their opponent will break down sooner or later. The key is to not let the level of your game fall even though you are temporarily losing points due to your opponent's hot streak.

Summary

This chapter has attempted to demonstrate the critical role that confidence has in our performance. Having a strong belief in your mental and physical abilities is essential if you expect to reach your potential. Confidence involves the way you think, feel, and act. Because these are so closely tied together it is important that you maintain your confidence in each of these areas. You should always strive for a strong sense of confidence without becoming overconfident or underconfident. You will not be confident every time you go out onto the court, but you need to strive to maintain a belief in yourself. You can do this by using some of the suggestions concerning building confidence in a systematic manner.

CHAPTER 11

Psychological Skill #6: Motivation Through Goal Setting

Motivation depends in a very large part on goal setting. The coach must have goals. The team must have goals. Each individual tennis player must have goals—real, vivid, living goals. . . . Goals keep everyone on target. Goals commit me to the work, time, pain and whatever else is part of the price of achieving success.

This quote by a top collegiate tennis player captures the important role that setting goals can have on a tennis player's motivation. In the previous chapters I have presented several psychological skills that are important to improve the mental side of your game. Although these skills are an integral part of any mental training progam, without the proper motivation, desire, and commitment, you are not likely to follow through on your program.

Furthermore, if you are having motivational problems, there is a high probability that you are also experiencing some performance problems. Motivation is a powerful source of energy, and without it your progress will come to a halt. The game of tennis requires a great deal of effort, energy, and commitment, especially if you are truly interested in improving your game. The hours that are required for practice can sometimes result in a loss of motivation and desire, but it is not just the amount of time on the court that causes a decrease in motivation. Probably a more critical factor that determines your motivation is the amount of success that you achieve. This success is not concerned with how other people view or evaluate your performance, but rather how you yourself perceive your performance and progress. As long as you see yourself succeeding and moving toward a meaningful goal then the chances are extremely high that you will maintain a high level of motivation.

This brings us back to the critical role that goals play in your motivation and commitment to the game. Goals provide you with a sense of purpose and direction as well as stimulating you to meet challenges. As Keith Bell[1] aptly notes in his book entitled *Championship Tennis*, "*Floundering in the world of sports without setting goals is like shooting without aiming. You might enjoy the blast and kick of the gun, but you probably won't bag the bird.*"

The purpose of this chapter is to discuss the important role that goal setting can have in sustaining motivation and improving your mental outlook toward tennis. First, I provide a definition of goal setting and then identify how and why goals work. Second, I discuss guidelines for setting up a goal-setting program. Third, I present a goal-setting system for tennis coaches to follow. Fourth, I address some common problems in setting goals.

Definition and Types of Goals

In its most basic form, goal setting is the aim or purpose of an action. For most of us that simply means identifying what we are attempting to accomplish or achieve. In fact, researchers have defined a goal as attaining a specific standard of proficiency on a task, usually within a specified time limit. From a practical point of view, goals usually focus on achieving some standard of excellence, whether it be improving your first serve percentage from 50% to 55%, reducing your unforced errors from 20 per match to 10 per match, or winning a particular tournament. The definition of a goal also implies that these performance standards will be accomplished within some specified time period such as one a month, six practice sessions, or by the end of the season. Although the preceding definition provides a general description of what a goal is, it is useful to distinguish between different types of goals. For example, doing your best or getting into top shape is called a *subjective goal*. Winning the club championship or making the college tennis team is called a *general objective goal*. Finally, hitting 20 consecutive groundstrokes between the service line and the baseline in practice or achieving a 15-5 win-loss record for the season is an example of a *specific objective goal*.

Another distinction that sport psychologists have made recently is between *outcome goals* which represent standards of performance that focus on the end result or outcome of a competitive match (i.e., winning or losing), and *performance goals*, which focus on improvements relative to one's own standard of excellence (i.e., improving the consistency of your backhand). To a certain extent, outcome goals rely on the ability of your opponent, because if your goal is to win a match or tournament you might play very well but lose to a tough opponent and thus not achieve your goal. Conversely, performance goals have nothing to do with your opposition, and thus are only dependent on your own performance. These distinctions will become important when I discuss using goals to improve performance. But first I will explain how and why goal setting works in improving performance.

Why Goals Work

The positive effect of goal setting on performance is one of the strongest and replicable findings in the psychological literature. In fact, in 99 of 110 studies, people who set specific hard goals produced performance that was superior to people who did not set goals, who set easy goals, or who were simply told to do their best. On the average, setting goals increased performance by 16%. Wouldn't you like to improve your tennis game by 16%? Let us for a moment explore the reasons why goals have such an important effect on performance.

Goals Help Determine What's Important to You

One of the major ways that goals work is by providing you with direction and guiding you along your journey to success. It is easy to lose track of your purpose, especially if you are aiming for something long-term like getting a college tennis scholarship but are still three years away from entering college. Goals help put things in perspective; once you have established where you are going and what you hope to find when you get there, goals will help you find the surest, quickest route to follow. In essence, goals can guide you and help you succeed.

Goals Maintain Motivation

Tennis players are only able to reach their potential if they are motivated. Although most of us are motivated from time to time, goals help us to sustain our motivation over a long period of time. Sometimes when practice gets boring, you have a nagging injury, or you are fatigued, it is easy to give up and either quit entirely or just go through the motions on the court. The tennis player who has some short- and long-range goals will realize, however, that the drudgery, pain, and fatigue of daily practice will result in successful performances weeks, months, or even years down the road. By systematically outlining the steps leading to your long-term goals, you can readily demonstrate the connection between day-to-day behaviors and future performances. This in turn can keep you motivated over a long period of time.

Goals Increase Effort

When you set a goal for yourself that is important to you, you will generally put forth more effort to achieve that goal. So, if your goal is to be in the top 10 in the state rankings and you are currently number 20, then you will have to try harder to reach that goal. Most top tennis players practice for countless hours to reach their high degree of proficiency regardless of their natural ability. Setting goals pushes you a little harder and keeps you striving to improve. Nothing can replace hard work, and goals keep us working hard in both practice and matches.

Goals Direct Attention

One of the ways that goals help improve performance is by directing your attention to accomplishing the task. When you set a goal, it helps you stay focused on a course of action that will help achieve that goal. For example, if your goal is to improve the consistency of your backhand, then in every practice session you should focus on that aspect of your game with some specific drills and exercises.

Goals Increase the Use
of Relevant Learning Strategies

A final way in which goals can positively influence performance is through the use of relevant learning strategies. That is, when you set a goal you have to figure out how you are going to reach that goal. For example, if your goal is to reduce your unforced errors from the baseline from 20 to 10, how are you going to reach this goal? You might decide that you need to hit with a little more topspin to provide a greater margin of error than your present flat groundstrokes. Additionally, you may decide that you need to spend at least one-half hour each day in practice hitting just groundstrokes, trying to break your previous day's record of consecutive groundstrokes without an error. In either case, you are devising a specific strategy to help you reach your goal, and this will usually produce quicker and more effective learning and improvement.

Goal-Setting Guidelines

It is hoped that you are starting to realize the many ways in which goals can improve your performance as well as make your tennis experience more enjoyable. It would be misleading, however, to think that all types of goals are equally effective in helping your tennis game. Similarly, setting goals does not ensure that you will experience any improvement in performance. In fact, some research indicates that certain goals or goal-setting programs do not facilitate performance. The good news, however, is that sport psychologists with extensive experience in employing goal-setting programs have come up with several useful guidelines for establishing a goal-setting program. These guidelines and principles are discussed below.

Identify Your Goals

One of the first things you have to determine is what you want to achieve. I have found that there is often confusion and uncertainty among tennis players in deciding what their real goals are. Identifying where you want to go and what you want to accomplish as a tennis player sometimes requires soul searching. Younger players in particular need to sort out their own goals from the goals of parents, other tennis players, and coaches. The input from those people should not be disregarded, but players need to decide for themselves what they want to get out of the game.

One way to help get started identifying your goals is to ask yourself a series of questions concerning your tennis skills and attitudes about the game.

- What are my greatest weaknesses as a tennis player?
- What are my greatest strengths as a tennis player?
- What aspects of tennis are most enjoyable for me?
- How much time am I willing to put into practicing?
- Am I working hard or just putting in time?

- Do I avoid practicing shots that I need to work on?
- Do I prepare myself mentally for practice and matches?
- Am I in excellent physical condition?
- Do I understand the strategic aspects of the game?
- Are my shot mechanics efficient and effective?
- What kind of tennis player would I like to be in six months? In one year?

As you attempt to address some of these questions you will realize that the answers are not simple or straightforward. Thinking about these things will help clarify what you want to accomplish in tennis and identify some specific areas of improvement or emphasis.

Set Challenging Goals

One of the strongest findings in the goal-setting literature is that goals need to be difficult and challenging. Goals have a way of determining levels of performance. Just as aiming at a target helps determine the general direction in which you shoot, setting goals can largely determine the range in which you perform. In fact, research has demonstrated that the more difficult the goal the better the performance, as long as the goal does not exceed your ability.

Of course there are realistic limits as to what you can do at this point in time. But some goals put a limit on what you are likely to achieve. If you set your goals too low you might be satisfied with performance that is less than your best. For example, if your goal is to make your high school tennis team you might be satisfied just to make the team even if you do not get a chance to play in many matches. If you really worked hard, you might break the starting lineup, but if your goal was just to make the team then you probably would not ever improve enough to play in the matches.

Of course, there are times when setting an unobtainable or unrealistic goal can undermine your motivation and performance. This type of goal produces repeated failure and thus discourages you from continuing to work hard and improve. For example, if you are playing number six on your college tennis team, it is unrealistic to have a goal of making it in professional tennis. Tennis players in this position, however, often point to the fact that they knew a player who actually accomplished this goal. The fact that it only happened one time in a thousand does not seem to matter to the player. Players with unrealistic goals will most likely fail, which in turn reduces motivation and confidence.

This is not to say that you can't shoot for the stars. Everyone can dream of being on center court at Wimbledon, because for some players this dream actually comes true. You need to separate your dreams from the reality of your present situation. Your goals should reflect your ability and experience, but don't severely limit yourself or restrict what you might accomplish in the future. Keep your dreams, but set some challenging goals for the present that might make it possible for you to achieve those dreams in the future.

Set Short- and Long-Term Goals

When I ask tennis players to list their goals, they usually identify long-range objectives such as winning a particular championship, getting a college tennis scholarship, or achieving a state ranking by the end of the year. However, sport psychologists have emphasized the need for short-term goals in addition to long-term goals. Short-term goals are important for a couple of reasons. First, they provide you with feedback in terms of how you are progressing toward your long-term goals. For example, if your long-term goal is to be ranked in the top 10 in your state in one year and you are currently ranked 25, then you could set short-term goals of improving your ranking each month. Short-term goals can be goals that are accomplished daily. Some daily short-term goals might include hitting 50 serves, running three miles for conditioning, drilling on your volleys for 30 minutes during each practice, or hitting 10 consecutive backhands crosscourt without missing.

The point is that short-term goals allow you to evaluate your progress and alter or change your goals as the situation dictates. If your long-term goal is to play number one on your college tennis team by the end of the season and after half a season you are playing number eight you probably need to reevaluate your goal. It might be more realistic to readjust your goal to making it into the top six. Conversely, if you are reaching your short-term goals faster than you anticipated, you could decide to make your final goal even harder. Using the above example, if you reached number one by midseason you might set your goal at winning 70% of your matches.

Besides providing feedback to help you keep sight of your long-term goals, short-term goals also motivate you because you can see immediate improvements in performance. It is difficult at times to realize that all your hard work and sacrifice will eventually result in achieving some long-term goal such as receiving a college scholarship. But it is easier to maintain motivation if you can see some tangible results and improvements on a day-to-day, week-to-week, or month-to-month basis. Reaching your short-term goals reassures you that you are heading in the right direction and instills confidence that continued hard work will result in future success.

Set Specific Measurable Goals and Target Dates

Research has strongly indicated that specific, measurable goals are more effective in enhancing performance than "do your best" goals or no goals at all. The more clearly your goals are specified, the better they guide you to your long-term objective. Goals that are vague and unmeasurable are like poor directions which make it harder to find your way.

Unfortunately, many of us have been conditioned to think in general terms. As a result we tend to set goals such as improving serves, reducing unforced errors, becoming mentally tougher, or playing more aggressively. While all of these may be worthwhile goals, in their present form they are not very useful or informative.

Taking a closer look at these goals, what do they really mean? Does playing more aggressively mean coming to net more, hitting harder, going for the lines, or serving and volleying both serves? Does improving your serve mean hitting it harder, placing it better, getting a certain percentage of first serves in, reducing your double faults, or learning an American twist second serve? Does becoming mentally tougher mean that you try to improve your concentration, reduce your anxiety, build up your confidence, or spend more time mentally preparing for your matches?

As you can tell from the above examples, without clearly specifying your goals in measurable terms you become hard-pressed to know when and if you actually reached them. By using numbers to clearly specify goals, you enable yourself (or your coach) to measure your progress against the standard. In this way, you will give yourself a clear-cut means for comparing your actual performance to the goal you set for yourself.

Take the example of improving your serve. This type of goal does not provide any information concerning how successful you will be in actually accomplishing this goal. A more specific measurable goal might be, "I want to improve my first serve percentage from 45% to 55% in the next six months." You (or your coach) could then chart your progress and record your first serve percentage in all your matches. Or your goal might be to increase the depth of your second serve. To accomplish this, you might draw a line parallel to the serve line halfway between the net and service line. Each day in practice you would hit 50 second serves, charting how many you hit into the back half of the service court. Finally, you could have a goal of hitting 40 of 50 serves in the back half of the service court in two months.

By specifying your goals more clearly in terms of behaviors to be performed, you can break down larger goals into smaller more manageable units. This also provides you with an immediate objective that you can work on right now and brings you closer to your long-term goals. Be precise, state your goals in measurable standards of performance, specify the behaviors you want to perform, and set a target date to reach your goals.

Set Performance Goals Instead of Outcome Goals

In our society, success in sports is a highly valued goal, and many athletes spend a major part of their lives pursuing this American dream. When asked what being successful means to them, most athletes and coaches will usually say *winning*. In addition, they tend to set their goals in terms of winning since they feel that this will produce ultimate motivation. Recent research in sport psychology, however, has indicated that outcome goals (i.e., winning) are less effective than performance goals (goals relative to your own past performance). Outcome goals can be very motivating if you are playing a tennis player of equal ability. Unfortunately, much of the time you won't play against someone of equal ability but rather will compete against other players who are superior or inferior to you. This makes winning either too easy or unrealistically hard. So, if outcome goals are not really effective in helping athletes reach their potential, then why do most tennis coaches and players consider winning to be so important?

The answer to this question requires that we go look at young kids who are just starting out playing tennis. At the outset most young athletes raise and lower their expectations based on their own level of competence. Each success causes goals to be raised slightly to keep challenge high, whereas failure causes goals to be slightly lowered to keep success within reach.

As tennis players become older, they move into more competitive situations and find it increasingly difficult to control their own goals. Instead, parents, coaches, and teammates sometimes convey that winning trophies, coming in first place, and winning matches are more important than self-improvement and satisfaction. In fact, I have observed that many tennis players equate winning with success and losing with failure. These tennis players come to believe that if they win they are successful, competent, and worthy; whereas if they lose, they consider themselves a failure and incompetent. Thus, by equating their tennis achievement with their self-worth, these young players make competition a potentially threatening and stressful situation (see chapter 3).

Besides the pressure that outcome goals can produce, a second weakness is that, at best, we have only partial control over these types of goals. For example, your goal is to win a certain tournament. In the quarter-finals you play against an opponent who is really sharp and hardly misses a shot. You, in turn, raise the level of your game and play a wonderful match, only to lose a tight three-setter: 7-5, 6-7, 7-6. This result would produce frustration and anger because you were thwarted in reaching your goal: to win. Instead of congratulating yourself for playing one of the best matches in your life, you are forced to be upset by your failure to reach this outcome goal. Conversely, you might be playing poorly against an inferior opponent, but manage to squeak out a three-set victory, 7-5, 4-6, 6-4. Should you feel happy with your performance just because you managed to win (i.e., reach your goal)?

As you can see from the above examples, setting outcome goals based on winning and losing will usually result in problems concerning motivation and self-confidence. The alternative is to select goals that can make success possible for all tennis players. In order to do this, the meaning of success must be redefined. *Success should be seen in terms of exceeding your own goal rather than merely beating an opponent.* This is not to say that winning is unimportant; rather, winning should not be everything. In fact, winning should be considered secondary to striving to reach your personal goals. *These performance goals are not based on whether you win or lose but whether you reach a specific level of performance.* Performance goals, therefore, are totally under your control and they can be reached regardless of who happens to be on the other side of the net.

Research evidence, as well as interviews with athletes in many sports, indicates that athletes employ performance goals to maintain consistent levels of performance as well as to maximize enjoyment from their participation. There are many benefits that are derived from setting performance goals. First, performance goals make you responsible for your progress—you can't point to your competition as a reason for not progressing. You should take credit for your successes and accept blame for your failures. Second, your motivation can be maintained at a high level for your current skill level and your self-confidence can slowly build as you reach the goals you set for yourself. Third, because you don't have to worry about how your opponent is playing, you can concentrate and focus on your own game. You can control only your own performance and not the performance of other players. Performance goals only require that you put forth your best effort whenever you walk out onto the court.

I have spent a lot of time discussing the importance of performance goals. Now I will take the opportunity to provide some examples of performance goals. Remember that the number of goals is unlimited; the ones that you choose should be selected according to your current needs and abilities.

In matches
- Improving my first serve percentage from 50% to 55%.
- Reducing my unforced errors from 10% to 5%.
- Reducing my double faults from 3 to 1.
- Improving my successful passing shots from 30% to 40%.

In practice
- Hitting 20 consecutive groundstrokes between the service line and baseline without missing.
- Hitting 10 consecutive overheads without missing.
- Hitting 10 consecutive forehand and 10 backhand volleys without missing.
- Hitting 10 consecutive crosscourt backhands and forehands without missing.

Set Goals for Practice and Matches

Many tennis players make the mistake of only setting goals for what they want to accomplish in matches. Goals should also be set for practice sessions. Most good tennis players spend a lot more time practicing than they do playing matches. Although not incorrect, the old saying, "practice makes perfect," is better said: "Perfect practice makes perfect."

It is certainly true that daily practice can be boring, and it is sometimes hard to be motivated for each practice session. This is where daily practice goals can come into play. These goals can provide additional motivation and direction for what you need to accomplish. You need to try to accomplish something every time you go out onto the court. This can include things like working on your serve, improving your volley, getting in better physical condition, working on your return of serve, and improving your concentration. The main point is to set some specific, measurable goals in whatever part of your game you want to improve. This will help focus your practices so that you avoid hitting the ball around for an hour and not accomplishing anything.

Identify Strategies to Reach Your Goals

Tennis players fail to reach their goals for a variety of reasons, but one of the major obstacles is a failure to identify any useful strategies to help achieve the goal. Although a goal can provide you with direction, you still have to map out a strategy of how to get there.

Let us take the example of setting a goal to improve the consistency of your groundstrokes: You want to reduce your unforced groundstroke errors from 20 per match to 10 per match in two months. This is a good, specific, measurable goal. What do you have to do to realize this goal? At this point, you should identify certain goal strategies that will help you reach your goal. Some examples of these strategies are (a) spending an extra 15 minutes in practice working on your groundstrokes for depth and consistency, (b) hitting with more topspin to provide you with greater margin for error, (c) shortening your backswing to avoid overhitting, and (d) hitting more crosscourt shots because they have less chance of error than

Table 11.1 Setting Your Goals

1. Long-Term (dream) Goal

2. This Goal Can Be Broken Down Into The Following
   a) Intermediate Goals (monthly)
   b) Short-Term Goals (weekly and daily)
   c) Long-Term Goals (for this year or season)

3. Other Long-Term Goals

4. Target Dates
   a) Long-Term Goals
   b) Intermediate Goals
   c) Short-Term Goals

5. Strategies For Achieving Goals
   a) Daily Practices
   b) Match Competition
   c) Seasonal Plans

down-the-line shots. Try to identify what you need to do to achieve your goals.

Write Down Your Goals

At the beginning of a goal-setting program, many tennis players are excited about their goals; as time passes, however, it is easy to lose focus of what needs to be accomplished. Therefore, it is a good idea to not only write down your goals but put them in a visible place such as the locker room or on the wall in your room at home. Writing down goals also increases their clarity and provides a reference for all types of goals. In addition, the relationship of one goal to another becomes more clear when they are written down.

One way to keep an accurate account of your goals is to start a notebook that contains your written goal statements. One big advantage of this is that it provides you with regular feedback. As mentioned previously, this written feedback can serve as a powerful motivator to sustain your efforts over time. Your chronological records can be kept easily and periodically reviewed. Thus you learn to evaluate your own performance by showing progress toward goal attainment. This can be an important lesson: you learn to evaluate yourself and therefore need to rely less on your coach or tennis pro.

Writing down your goals also serves the function of increasing your commitment to these goals. Research has demonstrated that merely writing something down increases your commitment. Goals, in and of themselves, do not mean anything unless you are committed to them. Having a permanent record of your goals and the progress you are making toward them is one good way to ensure commitment, effort, and persistence. Tables 11.1 and 11.2 present guidelines to help you keep track of your goals.

Table 11.2 Goal Achievement Card

Stroke	Specific Goal	Strategy	Short-Term Goal	Target Date
Serve	Improve 1st serve percentage from 45% to 55%	Hit an extra 100 serves per day in practice	Improve 1st serve percentage every match	Achieve 55% 1st serves by July 1st

Complete Table 11.1 at the beginning of the season, stating your long-term goals and breaking them down into intermediate- and short-term goals with target dates and strategies for reaching them. Table 11.2 displays a way you can break down your goals and use a goal achievement card to track your progress in reaching these goals.

Make Goals Positive

In setting your goals, you can state them in a positive manner, identifying things to do or in a negative fashion, identifying things not to do. Although it is sometimes unavoidable to set your goals in negative terms, sport psychologists strongly recommend that, whenever possible, goals should be stated positively.

If, for example, you want to reduce your double faults do not set a goal to not double fault. Rather, set a goal to improve your second serve by hitting with more topspin to provide a greater margin for error. To use another example, instead of setting a goal to not miss your service return, set a goal as to how many successful returns you want to make. In both examples, it is much easier and more productive to focus your efforts on doing something than on not doing something because you are focusing on success rather than failure.

A Goal-Setting System for Coaches

Thus far I have discussed a number of goal-setting principles that are important to follow if your goal-setting program is to be successful. Those of you who coach tennis might be asking, "How can I implement a goal-setting program with my team or at my club?" Sport psychologists have outlined the essentials of such a system in detail. Basically, your goal-setting program should have three phases: (a) the planning phase, (b) the meeting phase, and (c) the follow-up/evaluation phase.

The Planning Phase

As a coach, you should begin the planning phase by thinking about what the season is all about, along with your expectations and priorities concerning your team as a whole and each individual player. It might then be beneficial to start thinking about identifying specific team and individual needs. Some of these needs include physical conditioning, sportsmanship, development of fundamentals (e.g., strokes), footwork, and improvement of mental skills.

After identifying your specific needs, the next step is to turn these needs into specific goals. This will take some time and careful thought; you want to make sure that the goals you arrive at are realistic for and appropriate to each of your players. You need to consider each player's individual potential, commitment, and psychological make-up. In addition, although you could probably identify numerous goals for your players, it is important to choose those goals that are most relevant to each individual player.

The next step is to identify possible strategies to facilitate the achievement of these goals. As discussed previously, setting goals without any strategies to reach the goals will probably result in failure. Therefore, before you meet with your team, you must have done your homework. Commitment and effort from the coach is a critical factor in the success of any goal-setting program.

The Meeting Phase

After carefully considering the specific needs and goals of your team and its individual players, the next step is to organize goal-setting meetings. At the first meeting the entire team should be present. Provide the players with some basic information concerning goal setting such as the different types of goals, the importance of goals, and, specifically, short- and long-term goals, and performance and outcome goals. Then ask your players to carefully consider the goals that they would like to set for themselves as well as for the general team. Too often, coaches do not allow their athletes sufficient time to reflect on what kind of goals they would set for themselves. That is why it is recommended that you give your players a couple of days to think about their goals.

Schedule a second team meeting within the next few days to discuss some of the players' team goals. It is important to closely examine these goals in terms of their specificity, relevance, and realistic nature. At this time, identify the strategies that will provide direction for reaching these goals. Team goals only should be the focus of this meeting.

It is a good idea to work out individual goals in one-on-one meetings with each player instead of in front of the entire team. Therefore, schedule a number of brief meetings, making sure you get around to all your players. In these individual meetings, set specific, measurable goals, recording them along with the strategies for achieving these goals. Make sure that you allow the players to have input concerning their specific goals; your role is primarily an advisory one. This will provide for greater commitment from your players.

The Follow-Up/Evaluation Phase

The final phase in any comprehensive goal-setting program is evaluation. Unfortunately, this is an often neglected aspect because coaches get involved in the season and tend to fall behind in their assessments of the effectiveness of their program. One way to ensure that at least some evaluation takes place is to schedule goal evaluation meetings periodically throughout the season. This is a good time to discuss the progress that the players and the team as a whole are making toward achieving their goals and, if necessary, to revive a goal that has been achieved already or cannot be achieved due to unforseen circumstances such as injury or illness. The process of providing the players with feedback concerning their performance can be a powerful motivator. If you provide this feedback in written form, you can maximize its motivational aspects. This might take the form of actual match statistics, or you can provide your own evaluation of how well they are improving in a particular area. It is important to follow through on your goal-setting program with evaluations; this shows your commitment and dedication toward excellence. Your personal involvement will provide a model for your players to follow and maximize the effectiveness of your goal-setting program.

Potential Problem Areas

In establishing a goal-setting program, it is not uncommon for some problems to arise. It is therefore helpful to be aware of these problems so that you can structure your program to minimize their harmful effects. A few of these common pitfalls will now be discussed.

Failing to Reevaluate Goals

A common mistake that both players and coaches make is failing to reevaluate their goals during the season. Research has shown that this problem is more prevalent when people are far from reaching their goals than when they have already met their goals. For instance, if players reach their goals before the target date, they will usually set new, higher, more difficult goals. However, if players are far from reaching their goals, they will usually not readjust the goal downward to be more realistic. Coaches and players should recognize this problem and understand the importance of reevaluating and lowering goals when necessary.

Setting Unmeasurable Goals

For some reason, many players like to set their goals in very general and unmeasurable terms. Perhaps they don't really know how to set goals; it is also possible that setting several general goals prevents them from experiencing failure. I have discussed at length the importance of setting specific, measurable goals. So, encourage your players to be specific about whatever goals they want to accomplish.

Setting Outcome Goals

I have discussed the importance of setting performance as opposed to outcome goals. For too many tennis players, however, the only goal that matters is winning. This occurs due to the tremendous emphasis that we place on being number one. This makes it especially difficult for both team players and coaches to adhere to their performance goals when all that seems to matter is whether they won or lost the match. Consequently, it may be a struggle at first to resist the temptation of putting winning first. Fortunately, soon you will realize that performance goals will produce superior performance as well as the most enjoyment.

Setting Too Many Goals

A common mistake in establishing a goal-setting program is to set too many goals. If you set too many goals, then it is difficult to monitor your progress toward each specific goal. In addition, you fragment your thinking by trying to do too many things; the result is that you do nothing well. It is hard to make significant improvements in all aspects of your game in a short period of time. A more effective approach is to prioritize your goals and focus on accomplishing the one or two that are most important to you. As you achieve these goals, then you can start to concentrate on your other goals.

Summary

As you have seen, setting goals is a complex endeavor because there are many things to consider. When correctly set, goals can be tremendously useful tools to increase motivation and improve performance. To accomplish this, your goals should cover the full range from daily or weekly short-term goals to long-term goals. These goals should be reevaluated periodically and readjusted if necessary. Your goals should include what you want to accomplish both in practice and in competitive matches. A goal should be stated in specific, measurable terms with a target date to reach it. The goals should reflect a plan built to program in a fairly steady progression of success. All goals should be under your control and reflect specific improvements based on your own standard of excellence. Finally, your goals should challenge you and push you toward the limits of your capabilities.

CHAPTER 12

Mental Preparation for a Match

I start thinking about an important match the night before. I visualize what the match will be like and that keeps me from falling asleep. I have a court in my mind and I visualize points. I play the points out inside my head as I think ahead to the next day.[1]

Chris Evert

My feeling about preparing for a match was always this: that I wanted to do as much as I could ahead of time to prevent distractions. I was a creature of routine. It was always important for my peace of mind to have gotten a good night's sleep the night before, to have eaten at the right time—early enough that I wouldn't be bloated, but not so early that I'd be in trouble if I had to play a four-hour match. I was very finicky about my equipment. I always had to make sure that my racquets were strung right, and that I'd gone out and warmed up enough to get a feel for the sun, the wind and the bounce. Other players were different—although even seemingly casual players, like Bobby Riggs, had their own patterns. I found that if I didn't make sure of all these things ahead of time, I'd start to think about them a little bit during the match and it affected my concentration.[2]

Jack Kramer

The above quotes underline the importance of mentally preparing yourself to play competitive tennis. Thus far I have focused on the mental techniques that you can use at home or during practice to maximize your performance potential. In many instances, however, matches are won and lost before the first point even is played due to prematch preparation or the lack of it. You have probably experienced times when your mind was so occupied by other significant events in your life at work, school, or home that you could not adequately prepare yourself mentally or emotionally for an upcoming tennis match. Sometimes, you might have had to rush from work or school to a tennis match. In these situations, you likely have not had sufficient time to prepare yourself mentally to play top-flight tennis. There are also times when you might have psyched yourself out in the warmup and gone into the match believing that there is no way you can win.

The focus of the present chapter will be to provide a structure for effective preparation and a way to avoid some of the common pitfalls of poor preparation. It is important to keep in mind that players need to develop the type of prematch preparation that best suits their personality, temperament, and physical conditioning. There are some general guidelines to keep in mind as you are preparing mentally for a match.

Importance of Prematch Preparation

Before we delve into the specifics of preparing for a match, let us spend a moment discussing the importance of preparation from a psychological and physical point of view.

Psychological Preparation

Besides the testimonies from tennis players, research has indicated that mental preparation plays an important role on the day of the match. The idea is to develop a plan that will continuously narrow your focus of attention as the match gets closer and closer. On one hand, most tennis players report that they do not have a consistent and systematic way of mentally preparing for a match. On the other hand, it is difficult to consistently play at the top of your game if your mind is not cleared of all other irrelevant information and focused solely on the upcoming match. Sometimes external events are beyond your control such as family concerns, business meetings, or school activities; but most of the time you can arrange things so that you can have adequate mental preparation for the match. Developing consistent routines is one way to provide structure to your mental preparation. These routines will be discussed in detail after I address the importance of physical prematch preparation.

Physical Preparation

Throughout this book I have focused on the mental aspects of tennis; but how you feel mentally is, in part, influenced by how you feel physically. For example, if you have an early morning tennis match and you had to stay up until 3:00 a.m. the night before taking care of an emergency, you will not be adequately rested, and it will be difficult to stay alert, physically and mentally. In addition, when you eat, when and how long you warm up, and when you stretch out are all important ingredients to a sound physical prematch routine. I will now discuss the different aspects of a good prematch routine.

Prematch Preparation

The most important consideration in a prematch preparation is to develop a consistent, reliable routine in terms of the mental and physical aspects of the game. Some parts of your routine might seem far removed from physically preparing yourself to play but just knowing that you will be doing this consistently before every match helps mentally since it is re-assuring and removes uncertainty. Let us now look closer at the general development of preparation routines.

Planned Routines—Getting the Winning Edge

It is important that the prematch routine you choose serves at least two purposes: to organize your time so that you can focus progressively on the match, and to remove uncertainty from your environment. If you don't prepare yourself to play a match, you are leaving room for distractions to enter your mind, thus impairing your concentration. This is why it is important to focus progressively on the match as it draws near. Allen Fox, a former NCAA champion and coach at highly ranked Pepperdine University, relates the following story of what can happen if you do not prepare for a match.

I was due to play Jon Douglas in the Pennsylvania Grasscourt Championship. I had beaten him twice already that year on concrete and now we were to play on grass which was Douglas' worst surface. I thought the match was a lock so I got myself involved in a two-hour chess game right beforehand. So I brutalized my mind through a

two-hour marathon and, when I got on the court to play Douglas, I felt
physically weak. Worse than that, I found that I was so emotionally
drained that I did not have the mental strength to concentrate for the
length of time it would take to win the match. Inevitably, I lost. I had
gone out there poorly prepared and had paid the price. Bad prepara-
tion begets bad results. [3]

Obviously, Allen Fox took his opponent too lightly and did not prepare himself mentally or physically for the match. It is not that unusual for tennis players to be lackadaisical in the way they approach a match. Getting ready involves being at the right tension level, feeling confident in your game plan, focusing in on the match, getting the proper rest, eating the right foods at the right time, stretching, and warming up. This preparation may seem like a lot to think about, but without it you are not likely to reach your potential.

The second, less scientific, but equally important reason for having planned routines is to remove uncertainty from your environment. As athletes, we are creatures of habit, preferring to structure things so that we repeat the actions that in the past have been associated with successful performance. In fact, many of these actions or behaviors appear to have very little to do with the upcoming match, but we do them faithfully anyway. In many cases, these actions might be considered superstitious. Tennis has more than its fair share of superstitious behavior. Although these behaviors appear to be useless, they serve the definite purpose of supplying structure when preparing for a match. Let us look at some examples.

Think of all the things you regularly do prior to or during a tennis match that have no apparent useful function. Some behaviors I have observed in other tennis players or have been told about include not walking on the lines when changing games or between points, wearing certain lucky shorts or a lucky shirt, always putting on the right (or left) shoe and sock first, making sure your last warm-up serve is not a fault, always wearing a wristwatch when you play, and always choosing to start the match on one side of the court (north or south) regardless of wind and sun conditions. What all these behaviors have in common is that tennis players associate their actions with successful performance, despite the fact that, objectively, how you play should not depend on whether you wear a blue or yellow shirt. But that is precisely the meaning of superstition—the misapplication of cause and effect. Somehow we have come to believe that not stepping on the lines between points will help us play better or, conversely, that we will play worse if we step on the lines. The following story illustrates this general point.

Tom Okker and Ray Moore were getting ready to play the semifinals at the Paris Indoor Championships. As they emerged from the locker room they began briskly walking side by side. Some observant spectators might have noticed that they were walking very briskly. By the time they were halfway to the umpire's chair their brisk pace was even further increased with each lengthening stride like it was a race. "*You bet it was a race,*" said Moore. "*It was a race to see who could reach his lucky chair first, although, of course, neither of us wanted to admit it. I had played well in that tournament, beating Vilas and Tanner, and on both occasions I had sat to the left of the umpire. Okker had been using that side during his matches as well. Neither of us wanted to risk breaking the routine, so here we were engaged in this farce of trying to reach a certain spot on the court before the other guy, when we were supposed to be walking calmly side by side. At the last moment, that bloody Okker broke all the rules and sprinted the last couple of yards so of course I had no chance. I mean the man's quick as a hare. I was livid.*"[4]

Although both players realized how ridiculous they looked racing for their lucky chair it was obviously important enough to them to carry out this behavior. Although you might think this type of behavior is absurd, in reality, it serves an important function. Specifically, these superstitions or routines calm your mind and give you confidence concerning the upcoming match. (Unless your routine is being broken as in the above example; that is why you should develop some flexibility in your routine.) It does not matter at all whether these actions relate to the actual match, rather the key point is whether you *believe* they are important. If you believe that putting on the right sock first will help you play better then it probably will. Logic has no place in superstition.

It is important to develop some type of routine and prematch structure that you can depend on, regardless of the situation. Some of this preparation might be based purely on what makes you feel good, whereas other parts should work specifically on doing certain things physically and psychologically to give you a winning edge. Whether it is the finals of Wimbledon, the finals of your club tournament, or just a competition match with your friend, the player who has devised a structured preparation is going to begin the match with a slight edge. When you walk out onto the court you want to feel that you have an edge; this usually helps your confidence and, subsequently, your performance.

There are times, however, when you will be unable to carry out your prescribed routine due to circumstances beyond your control such as a flat tire, family crisis, business meeting, or school commitment. Despite the fact that a routine can give you consistency, there is a potential drawback to placing too much emphasis on a set routine. If some circumstance interferes with your routine, it is important for you to be flexible enough to alter your preparation and still play well. You must be certain that dependence on your routine does not prevent you from playing well under adverse or unusual circumstances. As a preventive measure, it is a good idea occasionally to play practice matches without your routine. This will help you realize that you can play effectively despite not having performed your routine. Your routine should be designed to give you *more confidence* and make you feel comfortable. However, it is important to know that you can still play well if your prematch routine is altered.

Although you should develop your own individualized prematch routine, I will provide general suggestions concerning some of the areas that you might focus on in your preparation. Also, many of you might not have the time to establish a set prematch routine, but this section at least will provide you with a good framework from which to understand prematch preparation.

Game Plan

One of the areas that tennis players often overlook when preparing for a match is establishing a plan or strategy of how to play a specific opponent. Devising a game plan begins by analyzing and listing your opponent's mental and physical strengths and weaknesses, matching these against your own strengths and weaknesses. This task is obviously easier if you have played against your opponent before (which is usually the case). Try to picture your last match and ask yourself the following questions:

- Were you successful staying at the baseline?
- Were you successful coming to net?
- Did your opponent like to hit passing shots crosscourt or down the line?
- Did that person have any obvious weakness?
- How were your opponent's volleys?
- Where did that player like to serve on crucial points?
- How did your opponent handle lobs?
- Did that person have a tendency to become tentative?
- Did your opponent keep emotions under control?

Now take a realistic look at your own strokes and abilities. Unfortunately, many tennis players are not good at self-evaluation, and it is not unusual for them to think that they are consistent in areas where, in reality, they are not. You will be the best judge of whether this is true for you. For

example, having an exceptional day and hitting 15 aces and serving 70% first serves does not mean you can rely on your big serve as a weapon if usually you only hit about 5 aces and get in 45% of your first serves. Do not try to fool yourself; devise a strategy that you know you can actually carry out. The key point to a good strategy is to devise a plan that pits your strengths against your opponent's weaknesses. Decide how you can use your unique skills to your advantage, capitalizing on your opponent's weaknesses. In addition, consider how to protect your weaknesses from being exploited by your opponent's strengths.

Take the example of playing against an opponent who beat you last time by playing steady tennis and attacking your weak second serve. In this situation, there are a couple of points to consider. In terms of your serve, it might be beneficial to take a little off your first serve or hit with more spin to improve your percentage; as this will give your opponent fewer opportunities to attack your weak second serve. In terms of losing points from the baseline, you might consider attacking your opponent's backhand and coming to net, remembering that this particular player has trouble controlling his topspin backhand passing shot. Of course, the choices and decisions are endless: This is what makes the game challenging. It is sometimes useful to switch roles, pretending that you are your opponent who is preparing to play you. This can provide insight into the kinds of strategies your opponent might be planning for you and you can then devise some counter-strategies.

After you have developed your game plan, make a commitment to try to carry out your plan to the best of your ability. However, this does not mean sticking with your game plan if it becomes obvious that it is not working on that particular day. You must think about what you will do if your plan does not work and how you might change this plan. If you are losing 6-2, 5-1, it is probably too late to change your strategy. Conversely, if you lose a couple of points early by rushing the net, it may be premature to give up your strategy of pressuring your opponent's passing shots. Knowing when and how to reevaluate your strategy during the course of the match requires a lot of experience. Although changes will sometimes have to be made, if your game plan is well thought out it will carry you through a match most of the time. To go on the court, however, without a carefully constructed plan of action is inviting trouble. This all seems like a lot of work, but most serious tennis players find this process fun and enjoyable. It will also result in a more consistent level of tennis, and this is certainly one of your ultimate goals.

Eating

Although I have focused on psychological preparation, getting ready for a match also involves physical preparation. The role of diet and nutrition in physical preparation has received increasing attention in recent years. Many of the top players including Martina Navratilova, Chris Evert, and Ivan Lendl subscribe to fairly rigorous diets. It is beyond the scope of the present book to discuss diet and nutrition in detail, but some points will be addressed concerning when and what to eat prior to a match.

There are no exact rules to follow concerning prematch meals, although certain general guidelines should be followed. You need to figure out the best time for you to eat and the types of food to eat. In deciding when to eat, you have to consider how you play on an empty stomach (not having eaten in the last five hours) and how you play after just having eaten one-half hour before the match begins; it's best to find a happy medium between the two extremes. It has been my experience that approximately two hours before a match appears optimal. Anytime inside two hours may give you problems in properly digesting your food and converting it to energy for your muscular system. Conversely, if you eat five hours before the match you will already have depleted much of your energy reserves and might be hard-pressed to have the energy to endure a long hard match.

The following are some guidelines endorsed by exercise physiologists and nutritionists concerning the type of foods to eat and avoid before a match:

1. Avoid irritating foods such as spicy foods and roughage.
2. Avoid gas-forming foods such as onions, cabbage, apples, and baked beans.
3. Avoid fatty foods because they slow digestion.
4. Keep your intake of protein foods to a minimum.
5. Eat foods that are high in carbohydrates such as cereals or breads (with jam or honey) because they provide the major source for energy. The meal should be light to facilitate digestion.
6. Drink lots of fluids, particularly juice, milk, and water.

If you have to play early in the morning, and it is just not feasible to wake up two to three hours before the match to eat breakfast, consider the following suggestions. Research has indicated that no adverse effects will occur if the prematch meal consists of cereal and milk not exceeding 500 calories even if taken up to 30 minutes prior to the match.

Stretching

One of the things that sport scientists have learned in recent years is the importance of stretching out before vigorous physical activity. Playing competitive tennis requires you to be in top condition, and although many players work on their cardiovascular endurance, relatively few spend time increasing their flexibility through a series of planned stretching exercises. Stretching should be part of your daily routine prior to practice but it is even more important prior to matches, in which you usually extend yourself even further.

Proper stretching before a match can produce several benefits. One of the major benefits is that stretching helps to reduce the probability of injury. Injury is (or should be) a concern for players of all ages. Many talented young players like Tracy Austin, Andrea Jaeger, Jimmy Arias, and Aaron Krickstein have had their tennis careers dramatically altered or threatened due to injury. As you get older, it becomes increasingly difficult to avoid injuries when playing tennis. Tennis injuries include tennis elbow, back problems, stress fractures, shoulder problems (rotator cuff), heel spurs, and knee problems. Preventing or reducing the probability of injury is a complex process, but sport scientists and trainers have found that proper stretching can be an important aid to injury prevention. By stretching your muscles in a systematic fashion, you increase the range of motion in your joints which reduces the risk of injury due to overextending a muscle or joint.

A second important benefit of stretching is that, by increasing the range of motion, stretching can help your actual performance. In the serve, for example, it is important on the backswing to lay the racquet way back by extending your arm behind your head. If the muscles are tight, you will be unable to take your racquet back far enough which will reduce the speed of your serve. Flexibility increases your range of motion, allowing you to generate more power and to reach further which are both important considerations in tennis.

A third benefit of stretching is that it causes you to relax and release tension. As you learned in chapter 3, anxiety and tension can debilitate your performance; it is therefore important to effectively reduce your nervousness before going out onto the court. Proper stretching can reduce some of the tension and tightness in the musculature. Focusing your mind on the specific muscles that are being stretched can serve the purpose of eliminating anxiety-producing thoughts concerning the upcoming match. The details of the specific stretching exercises are available in various books on flexibility and fitness. The following are some general suggestions for you to consider.

1. Spend 10-15 minutes on prematch stretching exercises.
2. Perform all exercises slowly and gently, stretching to the point of perceived tension (static stretching) and holding for a minimum of 10 seconds. Stretching is most beneficial when muscles are warm, so try to increase circulation prior to stretching. It is also recommended that each stretch be repeated three times. After some practice, each position should be held for 30 seconds.
3. Include the major muscle groups involved in tennis such as lower back, calf, hamstring, quadriceps, shoulder, neck, and other areas that give you trouble.
4. Do not bounce when doing any stretching exercises.
5. If you are on a team, one of your teammates can help you stretch some of your muscles.
6. Breathe out gently when you are trying to stretch out a muscle; this furthers the relaxation process.
7. The above sequence should be repeated after the match to prevent muscle soreness and lengthen muscles that have tightened during the match.

Imagery

By eating right and stretching out you are getting your body ready to play. However, as this book concerned with the mental game, you now need to get your mind focused on the upcoming match. Specifically, you need to do the following: (a) bring yourself to your optimal level of arousal, (b) build up your confidence, (c) focus your thoughts just on the match, and (d) think about your strategy and game plan. One of the best ways to accomplish these tasks is through the use of imagery. As discussed in chapters 8 and 9, imagery is one of the most powerful mental devices you possess in your quest for excellence and should be included in your prematch routine.

One of the last things I ask tennis players to do before they go out onto the court is to imagine themselves playing the match. If possible, plan in advance to have access to a quiet room or spot where you can go through your imagery. Your imagery should serve at least three purposes: to reinforce your strategy, to get the feel of your shots, and to focus on the match. First, your prematch preparation is a good time to go over your game plan, reinforcing the style of play and shot selection you want to execute. If you want to attack your opponent's weak backhand, then visualize yourself in a baseline rally waiting patiently for a short ball. Then, when this occurs, image yourself approaching on the backhand side and putting away a crisp volley. Play out points in your mind as you would want to see them occur in the match.

A second purpose of prematch imagery is to just get the feel of your shots. See yourself hitting smooth and efficient groundstrokes; hitting aggressive, well-placed, crisp volleys; getting the rhythm on your serve; and stepping into your return of serve. This will also help you build confidence in your strokes and thus approach the match with a positive attitude.

A third purpose of prematch imagery is to focus your attention solely on the match. When you image performing in the match you are automatically concentrating on the task at hand. While you are blocking out irrelevant thoughts, you are focusing on the things you need to do to play well in the match. As the match draws nearer, most players start to get nervous and even psych themselves out. Imagery can fill an important gap of time with positive results. Be sure to follow the principles concerning the use of imagery presented in chapters 8 and 9. This should be the last thing you do before going out on the court to warm up.

Warm-Up

For all players, the last thing you do before actually starting your match is to warm up with your opponents. Most tournaments limit the amount of time you can warm up with your opponent to approximately 10 minutes. Many players find this too little time to properly warm up and, if possible, they try to find another court to warm up further. There is a great deal of variability to the length of the warm-up depending on player preference.

Most top players, for example, will warm up for as much as an hour before their matches. They usually shower and change clothes before moving on to the tournament court. But some players, like Guillermo Vilas, prefer to go directly from a practice court to the match court. He uses the practice-court time to focus his attention and to loosen up physically for the match.

Whether or not you have the opportunity to practice prior to warming up with your opponent, the warm-up should serve several purposes. First, during the warm-up period, try to loosen up and stretch out your muscles. This will be easier if you first go through your stretching routine. Trying to get the feel of the ball and fine-tuning your footwork and positioning are important in getting physically ready.

Second, try to find out the aspects of your game that are working best for you as well as those that are causing you problems. Accept the fact that a cue that helps you hit well one day may not work the next day. Similarly, a stroke that feels good one day may not feel right the next day. For example, if your big flat cannonball serve is not working, you might start off hitting more spin on your first serve until you feel your rhythm coming back.

Third, try to get familiar with the particular environmental conditions and court surface. If you have not played on the particular court before, take careful notice of the court's speed, reaction to different spins, slippery areas in terms of footing, distance behind the baseline, background, and any other peculiarities. In terms of the environment, the wind, sun, and placement of spectators are potentially important cues. I am always surprised to see that most players pay little attention to the condition of the wind (other than not liking it). A stiff 15 m.p.h. wind can have a profound impact on how to play a particular match. Different strategies and shot selection may be necessary depending on which way the wind is blowing. Hitting a lob into the wind, for instance, requires a very different stroke and follow-through than hitting a lob with the wind.

A fourth function of the warm-up is to evaluate the strengths and weaknesses of your opponent, especially if you know little about that person's game. Things to look out for include: Is your opponent right- or left-handed? Does that person hit with topspin or slice? Are his or her volleys crisp? Does your opponent move well? How are his or her first and second serves? You should also be trying to get used to your opponent's shots in terms of pace, depth, and flight characteristics. Of course, many tennis players try to hide their real shots during the warm-up, but you can at least get the feel for some of the things your opponent will do. It should be noted that getting yourself ready should be your primary function; analyzing your opponent's game should be a secondary function. Spending too much time worrying about your opponent could prove disastrous; this will be discussed in chapter 13.

The fifth and final function that your warm-up can serve is to put you in the proper mental set to play. This includes focusing your mind solely on the task at hand. One very simple, but effective, way to accomplish this is to really focus on the ball, getting familiar with its speed, spin, and trajectory. Focusing on the ball requires a great deal of self-discipline which is essential if you want to make consistent contact. Focusing on the ball also prevents you from getting anxious and worrying about the outcome of the match. At the final stages of your warm-up you should try to increase your confidence in your shots and your ability to perform these effectively in the match. Confidence should emanate from within you and should not depend on the ability of your opponent. So, the warm-up should serve to focus your attention on the match, build confidence in your strokes, and reach an optimal level of arousal. You now should be physically and mentally ready to play up to your potential.

Summary

This chapter has highlighted the importance of mentally preparing for a match. Many tennis players show up on the court without ever thinking about getting ready for the match. Most of the best players have a systematic routine they follow to take them to their emotional, mental, and physical peak for a match. Each of you should develop a routine that includes a game plan, a specific time to eat, a proper diet, stretching exercises, imagery, and a warm-up. There is no ideal prematch preparation routine; you need to experiment and find out what works best for you.

CHAPTER 13

Gamesmanship and Psychological Strategy

I would rather destroy my opponent's confidence by forcing him into an error than by winning outright myself. Nothing destroys a man's confidence, breaks up his game, and ruins his fighting spirit like errors. The more shots he misses, the more he worries, and, ultimately, the worse he plays. That is why so many are said to be off their game against me. I set out deliberately to put them off their game. [1]

Bill Tilden

I can't say exactly what it was but sometimes I could look across the court and see something in the other player's eyes that gave me a feeling he was worried about double faulting. So I would maybe shade over a little bit to my forehand on his second serve, and a lot of times he would double fault. I got to the point where I felt as if I had the power almost to will the double fault. [2]

Pancho Gonzales

The above examples clearly demonstrate that tennis is a mental as well as a physical battle. Most competitive tennis matches involve usually a test of one's skill and shot making ability against that of the opponent. Probably the more crucial test, however (given equal ability), revolves around the mental struggle that occurs within the player or the mental games that are played between players. The mind games that go on in a competitive tennis match are almost endless. In the vernacular, one classification of mind games is known as the psych-out. Psych-outs make players start thinking about their strokes or their game in general when they should be playing more by instinct. In a psych-out, it is not important what players think about as long as they start to think about something. John McEnroe and Ilie Nastase have been known to cause their opponents to think about their antics and emotional outbursts instead of concentrating on the match. This usually causes the opponents' smooth coordination essential for proper shotmaking to be disrupted and distracts their concentration, causing them to focus on irrelevant thoughts elicited by the nature of the psych-out. Consequently, the subtle but complex nature of the psychological interplay between tennis competitors has an important impact on the outcome of tennis matches.

When and How Mind Games Occur

Of course, the difference between good strategy and gamesmanship is often a fine line. The rules of tennis are very specific concerning the physical aspects of the game such as the height of the net, the length of the court, the scoring system, and size of the ball. When it comes to rules governing psychological conduct, the rules are not black and white. What appears to be bad sportsmanship to one player might be seen as good strategy by another.

Take the following situation. You are playing an opponent who is serving unbelievably well, and the aces are adding up. You are desperate to try anything to get back in the match, but you just can't handle your opponent's serve. After another big serve you say, "Boy, I've never seen you hit your serve so well." Suddenly, your opponent becomes conscious of his serve, whereas before he had been hitting it smoothly and instinctively. He might try to hit it even harder to show you that he really does have a big serve. In any event, this minor distraction causes him to start missing his first serve and allows you to get back into the match. Is this an example of good strategy or psychological gamesmanship?

This next example is something I have seen Jimmy Connors do many times. On a big point in the match with his opponent serving, Connors invariably looks down at his strings and takes lots of time before the point. His opponent is anxiously awaiting to serve, but can't because Connors is not looking at him and is apparently not ready. When Connors is finally ready he looks up to receive serve; by this time he has thrown off his opponent's rhythm. Is this an example of smart tennis or does it border on unfair play?

The answers to these questions are not easy, and this chapter will not attempt to address them. Rather, the focus will be on identifying the different types of psychological ploys that you might encounter (or even use) and providing some suggestions for countering these mind games. Although there are a variety of subtle techniques available, most have the objective of convincing opponents either that they are going to lose or that in some way you are superior. Let us now take a closer look at some of the common mind games used in competitive tennis. I will begin with games during the warm-up because mental games start the minute you walk onto the court.

Warm-Up Ploys

One of the prime times for using gamesmanship and psychological ploys occurs during the warm-up. This is particularly the case when facing an unfamiliar opponent but it can also be a time to work on the psyche of a familiar opponent. In a warm-up you attempt to evaluate your opponent's strengths and weaknesses along with any clues concerning that person's mental approach to the game. It is a time to gain a psychological advantage, and some players will attempt to gain the upper hand in any of a number of ways. Take the example that Allen Fox describes concerning a match with Arthur Ashe.

I was pitted against Ashe in an All Star match and I had a broken little finger on my racquet hand so I knew I would have to come up with a special ploy if I were to have a chance of winning. So I searched around for some psychological ammunition to work with and decided I had two things going for me. First, it was a nasty day that would require a lot of motivation to play. Second we were put on a court where virtually no one would be watching, which further decreased motivation. God! This is supposed to be a big match and they've got us stuck out here, I grumbled as we set off for the court. I adopted a lackadaisical attitude during the warm-up and looked thoroughly disgusted about the whole thing. From all this, Ashe could only conclude that I considered the match unimportant and wasn't taking it seriously. So naturally, he was not about to try if I wasn't going to try. At the time, Ashe hadn't realized that I always try. He got behind at the outset and could never quite gather himself together enough to stage a comeback. I won 6-3, 6-2.[3]

During the warm-up players can work on their opponents' psyche through the types of shots they hit, the things they say, or things they communicate nonverbally. Let's look at each of these psychological ploys.

Types of Shots.   One way that a player can psych you out is to not let you warm up properly. As stated previously, the warm-up is a time to get the feel of your strokes and fine-tune your timing and coordination. Preventing you from accomplishing this goal can leave you frustrated and angry. For instance, when you come to net to work on your volleys, your opponent could decide to work on passing shots giving you little opportunity to practice your volley. Or when you want some lobs to warm up your overhead, your opponent can hit lobs that are so deep that you can't reach them. Similarly, in hitting groundstrokes, your opponent can hit the ball wide so that you have to stretch and expend extra energy if you want to get in any practice, or your opponent might hit the ball short consistently so that you have to play most balls on two bounces. These tactics can be certainly irritating.

Besides not letting you warm up properly, your opponent could also use the warm-up as a time to seize a psychological advantage and sense of superiority through his or her shotmaking. Imagine warming up against an opponent who hits all your practice serves back for winners, hits groundstrokes deep and with good pace, and puts away all overheads and volleys crisply near the lines. You might come to the conclusion that you're playing against John McEnroe or Martina Navritalova and give up before the match begins. In reality, your opponent may not be capable of executing those same shots consistently under the pressure of a match, but it may not matter if this defeats you before the match begins.

Verbal Interchange.   Another way players gain an upper hand during the warm-up is through the comments and conversation they have with you. Many times, small, off-hand remarks can set the tone for the upcoming match. Your opponent's comments may take the form of putting down your game, indicating that the match doesn't mean anything to him or her, and lamenting about his or her physical condition. Here are some typical comments that you might hear during the warm-up in an attempt to gain a psychological edge and psych you out.

- *I'm really tired after last night, but I'll give it the old college try.*
- *It sure is hot out here—I don't know why I'm even out here.*
- *My back is still bothering me when I extend myself.*
- *Can you hit me some shots with some pace?*
- *These courts are in lousy condition.*
- *It sure is noisy around here.*

Nonverbal Communication.   Although most of us think that the main way we communicate with one another is through verbal means, research has indicated that 50% to 75% of all communication between people is nonverbal. Communication on the tennis court is no exception to this rule as lots of things are conveyed through gestures, movements, expressions, and attire. These forms of communication can take on added significance if you do not know your opponent but they certainly can be important even if you are very familiar with your opposition. Some typical nonverbal communication during the warm-up that is aimed at working on your psyche is provided below.

- Carrying out five racquets.
- Dressing in expensive tennis clothes.
- Dressing in cut-offs and an old shirt.
- Purposely not speaking to you.
- Purposely avoiding any eye contact with you.

During the Match

Once the warm-up is completed and the match is ready to begin, a whole new psychological mind-set usually commences. It is now time to get down to the business of figuring out how to win points and games. Of course, the physical ability of your opponent is critical, but most tennis matches also include a psychological struggle for supremacy. We will now look a little closer at some of the mental games people play to gain a psychological advantage.

Posture.   The way you carry yourself says a lot about the way you are feeling inside. Generally speaking, you do not want your opponent to know how you are feeling; it is important, therefore, to convey a confident posture even if you are feeling down. Walking with your shoulders slumped and head down conveys the impression that you have given up or are feeling down. A good player will pounce on this opportunity to take complete control of the match. However, some players seem to deliberately walk around with their heads down just to make you think they have given up, when in reality this is not the case. A good example was the great Australian champion Ken Rosewall. After many points, Rosewall would act as if he barely had enough strength to walk back to the baseline for the next point. His posture told you that he was a defeated player. But any opponent who believed that usually wound up congratulating Rosewall on his fine win. So, a counter to this mind game is to keep an upright posture regardless of the situation. Also be aware of the ploy of using a slumped posture to communicate that your opponent has given up when that person is, in fact, ready to hit you with all available artillery.

Slow Down the Pace.   In the course of a tennis match, there are usually times that one player is under more pressure than the other player. When your opponent is under more pressure than you, it is a good time to slow down the pace of the match because this will keep your opponent under the strain for as long as possible. An opportune time to do this is when your opponent is ahead and looking forward to closing out the set or the match. Although this may seem counterintuitive, in most cases the player who is ahead is under more pressure than the player who is behind. As in many sports, the athlete or team with an early lead will usually try to cling to that lead.

In tennis, for example, players with an early break of serve will usually try to guard that break because they know that if they hold serve they will win the set or match. In addition, players who are ahead are expected to win and if they falter, they may be said to have choked. Take the situation in which you won the first set and are up a service break 3-1 in the second set. What usually will go through your mind is that you have to hold on to the lead because you certainly do not want to go into a third set and either lose the match or be forced to work hard for another hour. Your goal is to get the match over with as soon as possible and get off the court. At the same time, it is not unusual to become a little tentative in your play as you cautiously guard your lead. Of course, at this juncture in the match you would be expected to win and therefore have little to gain by winning but an awful lot to lose by losing.

If your opponent is aware of all of this, that person will probably try to keep you out on the court as long as possible. Your opponent can accomplish this by walking very slowly between points and making use of the entire 30 seconds allowed. They can become very deliberate in serving and receiving serve. In addition, taking the full time allowed during changeovers will further slow down the pace. This slowdown in the action is mentally draining and can change the rhythm with which you are comfortable in playing. It should be emphasized that this type of gamesmanship is considered slowing down the pace of the match rather than actually stalling. The player is taking advantage of the rules rather than trying to stretch or break the rules. Changing the pace of a match is a good way to break up the flow and rhythm of an opponent.

Another way to slow the pace of a match is to actually slow down the pace of your shots. Most tennis players like to hit hard, crisp shots. It is usually more trying and mentally demanding to play against somebody who is hitting high, deep shots with no pace. This is especially true when you are ahead and need a few more games to win the match. Tracy Austin, who, as a teenager, was one of the top players in the world, often used this strategy to her advantage. Many players just want to get the match over with and don't have the patience to wait for an opportunity to attack the shot and come to net. Sometimes, just playing a few points slow with high ''moonball'' type shots will be enough to throw off and frustrate a player's game. Some players feel this is not really tennis, but a competitive match is a battle of minds and willpower as well as strokes. It may not look pretty, but if you can hit one more ball over the net than your opponent you are going to be tough to beat.

Compliments/No Compliments.   Another little game that many tennis players play involves complimenting or not complimenting their opponent's good shots. Tennis players, like most people, like to be complimented. They like to be told that they did a good job, looked attractive, or gave a good effort. Basically, people respond to any compliment that tells them they're a good person. This makes them feel acceptable to others and that what they do is recognized and worthwhile. Tennis players like to be told that they made a great shot, have a great serve, or really hustled. One way to prevent your opponent from feeling good, comfortable, and confident is to avoid acknowledging good shots either verbally or nonverbally. After your opponent makes a great shot, just go about your business and walk at your normal pace with your normal expression to start the next point. This tells your opponent that you're not impressed with his or her shotmaking ability and certainly are not upset or disturbed by it. Most players like to get some sort of a reaction from their opponents after hitting great shots. By keeping your expression constant and not acknowledging the shot, you show your opponent that you mean business on the court.

The other extreme to not saying anything to your opponent is to compliment that person a great deal, even on shots that were not great. I once played against someone who complimented me only after he hit a weak shot and I had an easy putaway shot. It was obvious to me that I did not do anything special, and that the point was won primarily due to my opponent's weak shot. The message was that the only way I could hit a winner was if my opponent set me up for it. This type of compliment infuriated me, and I became more determined to show him my great arsenal of shots. This usually resulted in overhitting and errors. I have since learned to block out condescending compliments and just go about the business of playing tennis.

Line Calls.   The nature of the game of tennis requires most players (except professionals and those playing in some sanctioned tournaments) not only to play a match but also to officiate it. This is sometimes a lot to ask, especially when there is a lot on the line like state and national rankings as well as high school and college won-loss records. There are, of course, some written and unwritten rules governing line calls, but this does not always translate to on-court behavior. For example, if players are not sure whether a ball was in or out, then they should give their opponents the benefit of the doubt and call it good. Or, if you *clearly* see one of your shots out on your opponent's side of the court you should call it out. Although these represent good displays of sportsmanship, at times, we all have been involved with players who do not abide by these rules. As discussed previously in chapters 6 and 7, line calls can be a major disruption to your concentration. Some players are keenly aware of this fact and use it to their advantage. It is hard for most players to maintain their cool when a couple of their good shots on important points are called out. However, there are other options available to you besides blowing up and losing your concentration.

The first thing you might do is ask if your opponent is sure of the call. If that person is sure, leave it there. You are at least letting your opponent know that you are aware of what's going on. If it happens repeatedly ask for a linesman when one is available. In the absence of a linesman, some people respond by also making bad calls. This is not advisable, however, because it is wrong from an ethical point of view and will usually result in a further loss of concentration as the player focuses on line calls instead of the match. Getting into an argument with the opponent is counterproductive and ill-advised. The best (although not the easiest) thing to do is to forget about it and continue playing. There are very few tennis matches that are decided by a line call or two. The better player usually wins and if you can keep your composure and play your game you will maximize your chances of being successful.

Distraction.   Another common ploy is to distract opponents and break their concentration. A typical type of distraction occurs when players have an emotional outburst on the court, berating themselves, challenging a line call, or becoming upset with spectator behavior. John McEnroe, Jimmy Connors, Ille Nastaste, and Pancho Gonzalez are four top players who have had numerous emotional outbursts on the court. Although most of these outbursts have little or nothing to do with their opponents, they often produce disruptive effects. Some players just get upset at themselves and react to it emotionally, regardless of the score or situation. Other players, on the other hand, are more calculating and choose their spots as to when they will argue a line call and throw a temper tantrum.

A prime time to try to distract opponents is when they are gaining control of the match or when they have a good opportunity to get back into the match. In both of these cases, your opponent is playing well and you are searching for something to break that momentum and concentration. A slight break in the action is sometimes enough to pull some players out of their rhythm and timing. In addition, some players start to get mad and upset when their opponent is carrying on a five-minute dialogue with the umpire protesting a line call. Of course, if a player tries to distract their opponents through their own antics, they need to make sure they don't distract themselves. John McEnroe is one of the few players who seems to play well after an emotional outburst. But in interviews, McEnroe has indicated that on the whole, his temper tantrums and emotional responsiveness have hurt his tennis performance and, in fact, prevented him from being the first American in over 20 years to win the French Open in 1984.

Avoiding or Coping With Mind Games

Although you may not be the type of player who wants to get involved with mind games or gamesmanship, you may not have any choice if your opponent insists on playing these games. If you are confronted with some of the situations just presented, it is useful to have your own arsenal of how to cope effectively with them.

Strategies and Techniques to Use

Along these lines, some general suggestions for avoiding psych-outs and mental games will be presented. You will notice that these ideas will draw upon the psychological skills discussed in previous chapters.

Self-Statements.   One of the ways to ignore the events going on across the net is to have at your disposal a list of positive or instructional self-statements (see chapter 7). These should be targeted specifically for dealing with the actions or words of your opponent. Consider the situation in which your opponent is deliberately hitting to the corners of the court for winners during the warm-up instead of keeping the ball in play. A typical response would be to get mad at this display of gamesmanship, which is exactly what your opponent wants you to do. Instead of getting uptight, use some self-statements such as "If she is resorting to this type of behavior she must feel inferior to me," or "If I'm not getting warmed-up, neither is he." The main point is to stay calm and rational and not let the antics of the other player force you into playing his or her game. Develop a list of task-oriented and positive self-statements to deal with the typical mind games you are exposed to.

Focus on Concentration.   One of the main goals of most forms of gamesmanship is to somehow break the other player's concentration; that is, to get the other player thinking about things other than playing well and winning the match. If you encounter this mind game, one way to maintain concentration is to avoid making eye contact with your opponent who is obviously trying to get your attention. Some players will stare down at the ground or readjust their strings while the other player is talking and carrying on. Another way to avoid getting distracted by your opponent's antics is to focus on task-relevant cues pertaining to your strokes and strategy. For example, you might focus on your breathing or on a cue word like *relax, forward,* or *move.* If your opponent is arguing with the umpire, talking to the crowd, yelling, or doing anything that distracts your concentration, do not become an active participant or even spectator to that person's display on the other side of the net. Now is a good time for you to think about your strategy and plan what you want to do in the upcoming games. Or, you can think about some particular aspect of your game that has not been working and try to find a way to correct it. The point is to keep your head in the match and not have your concentration broken by the antics of your opponent.

Plan in Advance-Imagery.   Another way in which to combat psych-outs and mental games is through the use of imagery. Using the same principles discussed in chapters 8 and 9, you can use imagery to prepare to deal with disruptions on the other side of the net. If you are scheduled to play an opponent whom you played before and remember that this person is likely to argue line calls or throw a temper tantrum, you can prepare yourself mentally to effectively cope with this distraction via imagery. Specifically, you can visualize yourself in a match where your opponent stops play to argue about a line call. See yourself ignoring what is happening on the other side of the net and not getting emotionally involved. Instead, focus on what you need to do in the upcoming games in order to maximize your chances of success. Also, you can visualize playing a new opponent. In this case, image some typical distractions like arguments, yelling at oneself, disputing line calls, and talking to the audience. In both cases, the principle is to maintain your composure and concentration throughout the distracting period. The power of imagery allows you to prepare for this situation in advance.

Cope With Psych-Outs in Practice.   Another way to effectively prepare for the different types of mind games your opponent might have in store for you is to practice under simulated conditions. One of the ideas presented earlier in the book was that your practices should try to simulate match conditions as closely as possible. If you only hit groundstrokes and volleys in practice but never work on approach shots, you will inevitably have trouble with approach shots in a match. The same principle applies to psychological preparation. If you always practice alone and then all of a sudden 50 people are watching you in a tournament, this can be a very stressful situation. Although you want most of your practices to be under normal conditions, you should occasionally practice under adverse conditions so that you are prepared for anything. This will help you to avoid being psyched-out by unusual circumstances or behavior. Below are a few examples of how you might set up some practices to deal with mentally trying situations (all of these situations require the cooperation of a partner to serve as your opponent).

- Play a practice match when there are people walking around the outside of the courts.
- Play a practice match with virtually no warm-up.
- Play a practice match and stop play a few times to argue a line call.
- Play practice matches in the wind and when the sun is in your eyes.
- Play a practice match in which your opponent really takes his or her time and slows down the pace.
- Play a practice match in which your opponent is constantly yelling at him- or herself.

Summary

This chapter has presented you with different types of gamesmanship and psychological strategies that you might encounter during matches and in the warm-up. It is strongly recommended that you do not do anything that would be contrary to the written and unwritten rules of fair play and sportsmanship. It is sometimes hard to distinguish what is part of the game and what is bad sportsmanship. A good rule to follow is not to do anything to people that you would not like them to do to you. However, there are lots of ways to get to your opponent mentally within the rules. You need to know how to use psychological strategy to your advantage as well as how to counteract your opponent's mind games.

 CHAPTER 14

Psychology of Doubles

The game of doubles has often been neglected in the literature and on the court, most notably since tennis singles provide the greatest individual recognition and the greatest prize money (for professionals). Many college, high school, and Davis Cup matches, however, are won and lost in doubles. Furthermore, as tennis players grow older, there is a greater propensity for them to choose doubles instead of singles as their primary competitive arena. This is because older players find it harder to move around and cover the court; the game of doubles also offers more in the way of a social situation which many players find attractive.

As both players and coaches begin to understand the importance of doubles, there appears to be a need for more emphasis on doubles instruction and this is no more readily apparent than in the area of psychology. Instead of having to deal with the relatively straightforward one-on-one situation of singles, a doubles team must cope with and strengthen interpersonal relationships while breaking down the harmony that exists between the members of the opposing team. For a doubles team to be successful from a psychological point of view, a complex interaction of four personalities and styles of play must be negotiated. This is a partial explanation for why some people are excellent doubles players and only fair singles players (or vice versa) or why a team of two mediocre singles players can sometimes beat a team of two more skillful singles players. Sometimes, a person's physical abilities are more suited for doubles (e.g., good serve, volley, and overhead); also, many players are better psychologically suited for doubles than for singles, especially in terms of their communication skills—doubles is first and foremost a test of communication between partners. Thus the focus of this chapter will be to outline the communication process, discuss potential communication problems, and provide suggestions for improving communication.

The Communication Process

If you are to communicate effectively with your partner, you first need to understand the communication process and the different types of communication. It is important to realize that communication consists of not only sending messages but also receiving them. Many of us are very skillful at sending messages but are often weak at receiving them. Receiving messages involves good listening skills and you need to be able to be a good listener as well as a good talker.

Communication consists of both verbal and nonverbal elements. Although the verbal aspect receives the greatest attention, the nonverbal aspect of communication is as important and will receive equal treatment here. In most every message that is sent, there are two parts: content and emotion. The content refers to the substance of the message whereas the emotional aspect refers to the feeling about the message. In most situations, the content of the message refers to what you say (verbal) and the emotion of the message refers to how you say it (nonverbal). Because the nonverbal form is often neglected, let us take a closer look at this aspect of communication.

Researchers who study communication have found that approximately 50% to 75% of all communication is nonverbal. Nonverbal communication takes the form of gestures, facial expressions, posture, eye contact, dress, and tone of voice. For example, if you are playing doubles and you just double-faulted twice in a row, your partner might say "Hang in there, it's all right" while simultaneously shaking her head in disgust, which gives the verbal message a very different meaning. In our society, most of us are taught not to deliberately say something that might hurt another person's feelings. We generally are not taught to communicate through nonverbal means although many times it is our expressions, gestures, and postures that provide the true meaning to our message. That is why it is extremely important for us to understand how we communicate nonverbally; we want our partners to receive the true message that we send to them. I will address this issue again later in the chapter, but now I will focus on how to choose a partner.

Choosing a Partner

In doubles, one of the most often asked questions concerns how to choose a partner. This is not as simple a task as it seems because you must consider a variety of issues. First, you need to decide on what type of partner to choose in terms of physical skills. The basic principle here is to choose someone whose strengths and weaknesses complement your own. This presents a balanced attack and adds versatility and flexibility to your game. For example, if you are a steady player who keeps the ball in play, makes few unforced errors, but rarely puts the ball away, it might be well-advised to find a partner who has some big shots and can finish off a point, even though that player might be inconsistent at times. This combination allows your consistent play to keep rallies alive and provides opportunities for your partner to put the ball away; your partner feels free to go for big shots, knowing that you won't miss many on your side.

Besides choosing a partner based on shot-making abilities, it is also important to consider that person's psychological make-up. Don't make the erroneous assumption that you should be good friends with your doubles partner. In fact, it is not a prerequisite that you have to be friends off the court. Rather, it is more important that you communicate well and complement each other psychologically on the court. When the match gets tight and the pressure is on, you certainly do not want to become irritated with your partner; this is just the type of situation that brings out personality differences. Conflict most likely arises if both players want to take control and assume leadership positions within the team. Harmony can exist if one partner doesn't mind taking instructions from the other. The key is to harness the differences that exist between you and your partner and to make them work to produce a stronger psychological unit.

Communicating With Your Partner

As suggested above, the core of good doubles play is effective communication between you and your partner. During the heat of the battle nerves can get jumpy and tempers can flare, so here are some suggestions to help you communicate more effectively with your partner.

Be Supportive and Understanding.   The most important aspect of communication in doubles is to give your partner your total emotional and psychological support. To accomplish this you have to be sensitive and aware of your partners needs and psychological characteristics. Remember that your ultimate goal is to communicate with that person in a manner that facilitates the highest level of playing ability. The two of you are a unit, and you need each other's support and understanding to withstand the pressures of a tough match. This does not mean that you patronize your partner: False praise can certainly backfire. You should communicate that you are behind and have complete faith in your partner at all times.

Help Build Your Partner's Confidence.   In chapter 10, I stressed the critical role that confidence has in successful tennis. This factor assumes an added importance in doubles because when you make an error or blow an easy put-away, you are letting not only yourself but also your partner down. Although the overall pressure in doubles may not be as great as it is in singles, there are pressure-packed moments in a doubles match. For example, you are playing the ad court and the score is 6-5 with your opponents serving for the set. Three times in a row your partner wins the deuce point but you follow with missed service returns that would have evened the match. Not only do you feel bad, but also you are concerned that your partner is being brought down by your inept play. You also begin to feel guilty for holding your partner back and not carrying your fair share of the load. This type of situation wears down the confidence of most players.

In doubles, it becomes even more important for you to keep up not only your confidence but also your partner's confidence. Unfortunately, the situation occurs all too often in which one partner who is playing better becomes detached (consciously or unconsciously) from the partner who is playing poorly. Becoming detached protects the ego of the partner playing well who doesn't want to be associated with someone who can't get a ball on the court. The worse your partner gets the greater the tendency for that person to become isolated. This happens a great deal at the club level, but rarely with professionals: The pros know the importance of good communication and support. If partners don't have and don't show confidence in one another then their chances of success as a team are greatly diminished.

So, when your partner is spraying the ball all over the court, double faulting, and missing serving returns, it is especially important for you to express your confidence in that person. This can be done, verbally or nonverbally, in a variety of ways. This is where knowing your partner well is essential because you need to know the right buttons to push to keep confidence from completely disintegrating. For some partners, you might offer a word of encouragement; others might need you to tell them to relax; sometimes telling a joke lightens up the atmosphere, but there are also times when you should say nothing at all. The appropriateness of a given response depends on the situation and personality of your partner. Conversely, being overly concerned with your partner's play can distract you from concentrating on your own game.

Avoid Talking Too Much.   Although you must communicate with your partner, as a general rule, keep your conversation to a minimum. There is a tendency to talk too much, especially if you are good friends and enjoy each other's company. This can be costly if it distracts you from the business of winning the match. Limit communication to specific strategies (e.g., how you want to play the next point). A good doubles team generally involves knowing what your partner is thinking. Talking too much just throws your concentration off. If talking helps to relieve your partner's anxieties, however, then you should allow that person to talk to take off some of the pressure.

Be Honest.   Honesty is essential to a strong relationship between two people. Because most tennis players know when they're playing poorly, receiving compliments from their partners will only annoy them. Being honest doesn't mean saying that your partner made a terrible shot. Rather, it means that you feel comfortable with each other and are not afraid to say how you feel.

Honesty is also important in discussing your relative strengths and weaknesses. Tell your partner what your best and worst shots are. You also need to talk about whether you like to play the net and whether you are more comfortable returning serve on the deuce or ad court. Several doubles teams fall apart because players let their egos stand in the way of identifying their weaknesses and strengths. They won't admit that their backhand return is weak, second serve is poor, or overhead is inconsistent. Good doubles teams realistically evaluate their own relative skills so that they can maximize their combined skills.

Besides being honest about your physical strengths and weaknesses, it is also important to be honest about your psychological needs. You and your partner need to communicate to each other the answers to the following questions:

- Do you need a lot of encouragement?
- Do you like to talk a lot?
- When do you become most uptight?
- How do you respond to criticism?
- What should your partner say after a mistake?
- What helps build your confidence?
- What types of behavior irritate you?

Do Not Apologize for Errors.   Doubles players often ask me what they should do after they miss an easy shot. Some feel an apology is necessary because they are guilty for letting their partner down. Others don't want to say anything and just continue playing. Although apologizing is a natural thing to do after making a mistake (we are taught that to apologize after making a mistake is considered good manners), this rule of etiquette should not apply to the game of doubles for the following reasons.

First, apologizing only focuses both of your attentions on the error. You both know that you just double-faulted, and there is no reason to highlight that fact.

Second, apologizing for your errors is detrimental to your own confidence and will only serve to build the confidence of your opponents. It is bad enough that you missed an easy shot, but talking about it erodes your confidence even more. In some situations, you start to think that all you're doing is apologizing for your bad play, and this will serve only to make you feel even more guilty for letting your partner down. In addition, showing that you are upset and concerned about your errors and weaknesses will boost the morale of your opponents.

Third, constantly apologizing for your errors only confirms the fact that you are not playing well and pulling down the team. It's almost as if you wanted your partner to feel sorry for you because you are such an inept player. Usually, this only causes your partner to become irritated with you, and causes you to feel sorry for yourself even more. The best advice is to keep quiet after a mistake and concentrate on winning the next point.

Compliment Good Shots. Up to this point we have been focusing on how to communicate when one of you is playing poorly. It is also important to communicate when your partner is playing well. As mentioned previously, most players like to be told that they are appreciated and to know that their partner is aware of their good shots. This does not mean complimenting your partner after every hit. When your partner wins a key point or hits a good shot, reinforce that person's confidence by saying: "Great shot," or "Way to go," or "Way to hang in there." Something brief and to the point is sufficient. You both will feel better about your game, and you will feel good about helping to keep your partner's confidence up.

Know Your Partner's Tendencies. Communication between partners involves much more than what you say to each other. A good doubles team player knows what the other player is thinking. This is especially important when you are trying to predict what type of shot your partner will hit in a given situation as this can dictate your next response. For example, if your partner is receiving a second serve, and you expect that person to chip and charge after most second serves, you might crowd the net a little more and be ready to make a volley. Conversely, if you know your partner has trouble with American twist second serves and tends to float them back, you may decide to move back to the baseline in a defensive position.

Of course this unspoken communication usually takes a little time to achieve. Thus it is important to pay close attention to the types of shots your partner chooses in different situations. In addition, talking to each other before a match and sharing tendencies and plans will give each partner a better feel for what to expect from the other. In the heat of battle there is sometimes not much time for formal communication, and instinct is what guides play. This instinct can be developed over time if two players communicate with and trust each other. The idea is to work as a unit, be able to cover up for each other's mistakes, and, ultimately, make the two of you as a team better than you are individually.

Be Aware of Nonverbal Communication.   Earlier in the chapter, the point was made concerning the importance of nonverbal communication. Because you are often unaware of the nonverbal messages you send, this becomes a critical issue when communicating with your doubles partner. Playing competitive tennis can be very stressful, and although we can sometimes refrain from verbally expressiong how we feel, it is not as easy to hold back our nonverbal messages. If your partner is playing poorly in a match that you really want to win, it may be all you can do to maintain verbal encouragement. But, if you're walking around with a scowl on your face, shoulders slumped, and head down your partner is going to get the message that you're really upset with the poor play. It is very important that you are aware of not only what you say but also how you say it and how you look. This sustains your partner's confidence that you are supportive and confident, and at the same time lets your opponents know that you're both still mentally and emotionally in the match.

Improving Your Communication

Thus far I have discussed a variety of things to consider when communicating with your partner both on and off the court. If you want to improve your communication skills, you need to pay close attention to what you are doing and saying. The following are some suggestions to become aware of and improve your communication skills.

Log Books—Increase Awareness.   One of the best ways to make you more conscious of your communicating patterns is to keep a log book. The act of writing something down usually increases awareness. This is why one of the first things psychologists tell people who want to lose weight is to keep a food diary. This automatically increases their awareness of what they are eating. The same principle applies to becoming sensitive to your communication behavior on the tennis court by keeping a communication log book. The following are questions to ask yourself and record in your log book after a doubles match.

- When did I communicate well?
- What would I have liked to communicate?
- What would I have wanted to be communicated to me?
- Did I use criticism?
- What did I communicate nonverbally?
- In what situations did I communicate poorly?

Imagery.   Once again imagery is a tool that can be used to help improve your communication. The same principles apply as discussed previously, but in this case you focus on your communication patterns rather than your physical performance. Let's say that you have a tendency to give your partner instructions when he or she is playing poorly despite the fact that your partner has told you not to comment in this situation. Thus you might image a situation in which your partner is playing poorly; instead of instructions, you give some positive reinforcement to boost that person's confidence in the form of nonverbal cues like posture, eye contact, and gestures. The main point is to visualize yourself communicating in a manner that will help you both. This will become easier as you learn to talk to your partner and keep a log book.

Role Playing. Role playing is a technique that is widely used when communication between people breaks down or falters. This involves trying to empathize with, or take the point of view of, the other person. The objective is to vicariously experience what your partner is going through.

In a situation where your partner becomes more upset because you try to give instructions on how to play better, role playing puts you in your partner's shoes. How would you feel if, the minute you made a mistake, your partner started telling you how to hit your shots? You would probably be put off, even though you know your partner's intentions were good. Role playing helps you see your partner's point of view and gives you a better understanding of that person's feelings and actions.

Disrupting Your Opponent's Communication

Thus far I have focused on how to improve communication between you and your partner. The other aspect to communication skills in doubles concerns how you go about disrupting the communication between your opponents. You can accomplish this well within the rules of the game. The following are some examples of ways to break down the communication of your opponents and confuse their thinking.

Play to the Weaker Player. If one of your opponents is definitely weaker than the other, then attack that person immediately and often. This will not only win points but, psychologically, often cause a rift between your opponents. By hitting to the weaker player you are announcing that you have found your opponents' weak link and are intending to exploit it. This can serve two purposes. First, it erodes the confidence of the weaker player, making that person feel that they are holding back their partner. Particularly, as the weak player misses more shots, the pressure increases, causing a further decline in that player's performance. Second, it can make the better player feel burdened with the responsibility of coming up with great shots to win a point. Usually, this causes the stronger player to go for too much on serves and service returns, thus producing more errors.

It should be pointed out that playing almost exclusively to the weaker player can backfire. Remember that the game of doubles usually dictates where the highest percentage shot should be hit regardless of the abilities of the opponents. For example, let's say that the stronger of your opponents is serving. The basic shot would be to chip the return at the feet of the oncoming server. But, because you want to play the weaker partner you decide to pass down the line. This is generally not a good percentage play for three reasons: (a) the net is higher in the alley, (b) you have less court to hit in, and (c) it provides more angle for the volley of the person playing the net. As a result you hit the ball into the net. If you try to hit other than your normal high percentage shots just to hit to the weaker opponent, you can disrupt your own game and quickly break your own morale. Carefully select the appropriate time to play the weaker player. For example, if both your opponents are at net and you and your partner are back at the baseline, you might hit all your passing shots to the weaker player because this doesn't lower your percentage yet it puts pressure on the weak player.

Make Your Opponents Think. One of the big mistakes that doubles teams make is to play a very predictable type of game. They always hit their returns crosscourt and their first serves down the middle, and they play in a standard formation. This is not necessarily bad; rather, these are probably good things to do most of the time. Good doubles teams, however, vary their shots to keep their opponents guessing and to prevent their opponents from getting into a rhythm or style of play. You should especially vary your game if you are behind or if your opponents are doing certain things very well. A couple of examples will illustrate this point.

Let's say that your opponent's crosscourt returns from the ad court are consistently hard and low at your feet causing you to lose lots of points. What your team needs to do is try to disrupt the returner's groove. This can be accomplished in a couple of ways. One is to have your partner at net poach and try to pick off this crosscourt return. If this can be executed successfully just once or twice, it will start to weigh on the mind of the returner causing that person to make the shot too fine or try to go down the line. In either case, your opponent has to start thinking about an alternative shot to hitting it crosscourt. A second technique is to use the Australian formation with the net person on the same side as the server. This prohibits the crosscourt shot and causes the player to hit the more difficult down-the-line shot. Another formation that is just starting to catch on is called the "I formation." The net player starts right in the middle of the court and either moves to the right or left after the serve is put into play. Thus, on every point, the returner does not know which way the net person will go which makes it hard to get into a rhythm. In this way, you can get into a guessing game with your opponents, and that's exactly what you want to occur.

The main point is to make your opponents think about what you are going to do. Not knowing what you will do makes it harder for your opponents to communicate with each other. By causing uncertainty you break down their communication and coordination. Of course, you need to practice these formations and shots to make them work in a match. But if you can vary your game, be flexible, and keep your opponents guessing you will have gone a long way to winning the match.

Mixed Doubles

Thus far I have been discussing situations in either women's or men's doubles. Mixed doubles has become increasingly popular in recent years, and some of the unwritten rules are different from men's and women's doubles. I will now discuss the unique situation when a man and woman team up for doubles.

In playing mixed doubles, one big difference that usually (although not always) occurs is that one player is superior in skill to the other player. The other difference that may occur is that many times a mixed doubles team is romantically involved (e.g., husband and wife), and we all know how difficult it sometimes can be to play with those we love. Let us look more closely into how these differences can affect communication patterns and styles of play.

When a man and woman team up, it is typical that the male is the stronger player. Because men generally have more strength, particularly upper body strength, they are in a position to end points more often with an overhead, serve, or volley. In fact, the best strategy in mixed doubles is for the woman to play consistently and keep the ball in play while the man tries to put the finishing touches on the point by hitting winners. Inequality in ability sometimes translates to uneven and biased communication. Because the man may feel superior (whether he actually is or not) he takes it upon himself to dictate and control the communication. He may tell the woman where to position herself, what strategy to use, and how to hit certain strokes. This unfortunate situation continues when one player may feel pressure to win the points and dominate the game. The other player may then become afraid of making mistakes and stay positioned in the alley where there are fewer shots to hit and less pressure to make an error.

It should be remembered that mixed doubles, above all, should be fun. It is a time to continue learning and refining your skills. Regardless of the fact that there might be ability differences, communication should be on an equal level. The less skilled players should not allow themselves to be dominated and controlled. They should let their partners know that the only way to learn the game is by making mistakes and not by standing in the alley letting their partners take all the shots. In essence, both players are an important part of the team. Of course, these concerns should be addressed before ever stepping out onto the court because they are tough to resolve during the heat of a match.

It is also important to keep the match in perspective. In the long run, mixed doubles will be more enjoyable if both partners contribute to the team's success. Both players should show confidence in each other. Just because the male might be the stronger player does not mean that he should dominate his partner. In some situations, even if the woman is the more skilled player, the man may still try to dominate the play because he feels threatened. The goal, as in any doubles match, is to work together and pool respective abilities. If one partner feels incompetent, lacks confidence, and is intimidated by the other's presence, then that partner most likely will not significantly contribute to the team. It should be noted that although a woman may not be as physically strong as her male partners, she may have a stronger mental game, thus neutralizing any perceived differences. Even if you lose the match, you both have learned some things and experienced new situations which will help in your next match. Despite differences in skills, try to communicate as equals.

The second reason why mixed doubles is especially hard on communication is that, in many cases, the partners are romantically involved. This puts an added strain on things because it is sometimes hard to separate what goes on in a match from the rest of your relationship. Giving your spouse instructions may be interpreted as being bossy or showing displeasure, which in turn makes your spouse mad or upset and leads to an argument. I have noticed that nonverbal communication is especially strong in mixed doubles with romantically involved partners, specifically in terms of the man expressing displeasure with his partner's poor play. As in regular doubles, however, it is crucial to be supportive and provide maximum psychological support. Do not get caught up putting your egos on the line during a mixed doubles match. Maintaining a good relationship with your partner is more important than winning any particular match. Moreover, if you are serious and interested in winning, supporting and building your partner's confidence will increase your chances of playing better as a team. Making your partner feel incompetent and uneasy will result in tentative play and poor communication. Try to establish an atmosphere of open communication and support; this will not only maximize your chances of winning but also make your time together after the match more enjoyable.

A final point that makes mixed doubles psychologically different is that the basic strategy in doubles is to play to the weaker player, who, in many cases, is the woman. This puts the man in somewhat of a bind. Good strategy dictates that he should direct his shots to the opposing weak link, but there is also an unwritten social rule concerning how vigorous he can be in directing his attack at the woman. If he continually wins points by hitting hard shots to the woman, then he is open to criticism that he is taking undue advantage of her. If he tries to let up on his shots when hitting to the woman, then he is prone to changing his natural rhythm and missing easy shots or letting up too much and losing points.

If you are looking for an easy answer to this dilemma, there is none. How hard and how often the man plays to the opposing woman depends on relative abilities and the competitiveness of the tournament. A good rule to follow is to play the type of doubles game you would normally play (not mixed doubles). This entails going for the percentage shot rather than constantly picking on the weaker player. In addition, if you pick on the opposing woman, it is likely that the opposing man will target your woman partner. This will lead to a heated, unfriendly game of tennis which defeats the purpose of most mixed doubles matches. Try to have fun, communicate well with your partner, and respect your opponents. Mixed doubles can be a fun, social experience if you can avoid some of the pitfalls I have discussed.

Summary

The game of doubles is complex, and one of the essential ingredients of good doubles play is communication between partners. Playing singles is difficult enough, but when you have to consider also the feelings and emotions of another player it certainly complicates the situation. I have given you some suggestions for communicating with your partner, probably the most important of which is being supportive and understanding. You must remember not to lose your own concentration when you're trying to help your partner. In addition, I have provided some ways for improving communication including log books, imagery, and role playing. Finally, I have addressed the special situation of mixed doubles, noting the added problems of having a male and female on the same side of the court. When the partners are also involved in a romantic relationship, this makes communication especially sensitive.

Reference Notes

Chapter 2

1. Tarshis, B. (1977). *Tennis and the mind* (p. 3). New York: Tennis Magazine.
2. Tarshis, B. (1977). *Tennis and the mind* (p. 53). New York: Tennis Magazine.
3. Dallas Morning News. (1985, September).
4. Tarshis, B. (1977). *Tennis and the mind* (p. 91). New York: Tennis Magazine.
5. Tarshis, B. (1977). *Tennis and the mind* (p. 91). New York: Tennis Magazine.
6. Tarshis, B. (1977). *Tennis and the mind* (p. 21). New York: Tennis Magazine.
7. Tarshis, B. (1977). *Tennis and the mind* (p. 32). New York: Tennis Magazine.
8. Tarshis, B. (1977). *Tennis and the mind* (p. 87). New York: Tennis Magazine.
9. Tarshis, B. (1977). *Tennis and the mind* (p. 76). New York: Tennis Magazine.
10. Gallwey, T. (1974). *Inner game of tennis* (pp. 50-51). New York: Random House.

Chapter 3

1. Tarshis, B. (1977). *Tennis and the mind* (p. 89). New York: Tennis Magazine.
2. Tarshis, B. (1977). *Tennis and the mind* (p. 63). New York: Tennis Magazine.
3. Tarshis, B. (1977). *Tennis and the mind* (p. 87). New York: Tennis Magazine.
4. Tarshis, B. (1977). *Tennis and the mind* (p. 159). New York: Tennis Magazine.
5. Tarshis, B. (1977). *Tennis and the mind* (p. 170). New York: Tennis Magazine.
6. Tarshis, B. (1977). *Tennis and the mind* (p. 170). New York: Tennis Magazine.

Chapter 4

1. Jacobson, E. (1938). *Progressive relaxation*. Chicago: University of Chicago Press.
2. Benson, H. (1975). *The relaxation response*. New York: Morrow.

Chapter 5

1. Tarshis, B. (1977). *Tennis and the mind* (p. 31). New York: Tennis Magazine.
2. Tarshis, B. (1977). *Tennis and the mind* (p. 21). New York: Tennis Magazine.
3. Tarshis, B. (1977). *Tennis and the mind* (p. 25). New York: Tennis Magazine.

Chapter 6

1. Tarshis, B. (1977). *Tennis and the mind* (p. 44). New York: Tennis Magazine.
2. Gallwey, T. (1974). *Inner Game of Tennis*. New York: Random House.
3. Phillips, B.J. (1980, June). The tennis machine. *Time*, p. 56.
4. Tarshis, B. (1977). *Tennis and the mind* (p. 45). New York: Tennis Magazine.

5. Tarshis, B. (1977). *Tennis and the mind* (p. 48). New York: Tennis Magazine.
6. Tarshis, B. (1977). *Tennis and the mind* (p. 40). New York: Tennis Magazine.

Chapter 7

1. Ellis, A. (1962). *Reason and emotion in psychotherapy.* New York: Lyle Stuart.

Chapter 8

1. Nicklaus, J. (1976). *Play better golf.* New York: King Features Syndicate.
2. Suinn, R. (1977). Behavioral methods at the winter Olympic Games. *Behavior Therapy, 8,* 283-284.
3. Martens, R. (1982, September). *Imagery in sport.* Paper presented at the Medical and Scientific Aspects of Elitism in Sport Conference, Brisbane, Australia.

Chapter 9

1. Hale, B.D. (1982). The effects of internal and external imagery on muscular and ocular concomitants. *Journal of Sport Psychology, 4,* 379-387.
2. Harris, D.V., & Robinson, W.J. (1986). The effects of skill level on EMG activity during internal and external imagery. *Journal of Sport Psychology, 8,* 105-111.

Chapter 10

1. Tarshis, B. (1977). *Tennis and the mind* (p. 102). New York: Tennis Magazine.
2. Tarshis, B. (1977). *Tennis and the mind* (p. 93). New York: Tennis Magazine.
3. Tarshis, B. (1977). *Tennis and the mind* (p. 90). New York: Tennis Magazine.
4. Rosenthal, R., & Jacobson, L. (1968). *Pygmalion in the classroom: Teacher expectancies and pupils' intellectual achievement.* New York: Holt, Rinehart and Winston.
5. Tarshis, B. (1977). *Tennis and the mind* (p. 94). New York: Tennis Magazine.
6. Weinberg, R.S., Gould, D., & Jackson, A. (1979). Expectancies and performance: An empirical test of Bandura's self-efficacy theory. *Journal of Sport Psychology, 1,* 320-331.
7. Weinberg, R.S., Richardson, P., & Jackson, A. (1981). Effect of situation criticality on tennis performance of males and females. *International Journal of Sport Psychology, 12,* 253-259.
8. Ransom, K., & Weinberg, R.S. (1985). Effect of situation criticality on performance of elite male and female tennis players. *Journal of Sport Behavior, 8,* 144-148.
9. Tarshis, B. (1977). *Tennis and the mind* (p. 92). New York: Tennis Magazine.
10. Tarshis, B. (1977). *Tennis and the mind* (p. 148). New York: Tennis Magazine.
11. Tarshis, B. (1977). *Tennis and the mind* (p. 102). New York: Tennis Magazine.
12. Tarshis, B. (1977). *Tennis and the mind* (p. 96). New York: Tennis Magazine.
13. Tarshis, B. (1977). *Tennis and the mind* (p. 134). New York: Tennis Magazine.

Chapter 11

1. Bell, K. (1983). *Championship thinking* (p. 64). Englewood Cliffs, NJ: Prentice Hall.

Chapter 12

1. Lloyd, C.E. (1986). Think success. *World Tennis, 34*(3), 38.
2. Tarshis, B. (1977). *Tennis and the mind* (p. 37). New York: Tennis Magazine.
3. Fox, A., & Evan, R. (1979). *If I'm the better player, why can't I win?* (p. 72). New York: Tennis Magazine.
4. Tarshis, B. (1977). *Tennis and the mind* (p. 52). New York: Tennis Magazine.

Chapter 13

1. Tarshis, B. (1977). *Tennis and the mind* (p. 119). New York: Tennis Magazine.
2. Tarshis, B. (1977). *Tennis and the mind* (p. 151). New York: Tennis Magazine.
3. Fox, A., & Evan, R. (1979). *If I'm the better player, why can't I win?* (p. 117). New York: Tennis Magazine.

Index